Sales Audit

Sales Audit

The Sales Manager's Playbook for Getting Control of the Selling Cycle and Improving Results

Corey M. Hutchison

iUniverse, Inc.
New York Lincoln Shanghai

Sales Audit
The Sales Manager's Playbook for Getting Control of the Selling Cycle and Improving Results

Copyright © 2006 by Corey M. Hutchison

iUniverse books may be ordered through booksellers or by contacting:

iUniverse
2021 Pine Lake Road, Suite 100
Lincoln, NE 68512
www.iuniverse.com
1-800-Authors (1-800-288-4677)

The information, ideas, and suggestions in this book are not intended to render professional advice. Before following any suggestions contained in this book, you should consult your personal accountant or other financial advisor. Neither the author nor the publisher shall be liable or responsible for any loss or damage allegedly arising as a consequence of your use or application of any information or suggestions in this book.

ISBN-13: 978-0-595-42134-3 (pbk)
ISBN-13: 978-0-595-86474-4 (ebk)
ISBN-10: 0-595-42134-2 (pbk)
ISBN-10: 0-595-86474-0 (ebk)

Printed in the United States of America

In Memory of Mom, Dad and Heidi

"The beauty of a life well-lived never dies ... it continues to embrace and inspire us"

This book is uniquely inspired by each of you

"Clearly defined and replicable processes are valued in many walks of life. A coach will have well rehearsed and demonstrably effective plays and game plans that raise the probability of winning. A general in military action depends on understood processes and established routines on which he can build success. Airline pilots and crews have carefully documented and well rehearsed procedures for dealing with almost any situation. Scientists won't trust a result until they understand the process that generated it, and can repeat that process with different people in different settings. We can always launch energetic sales people out the door and hope for the best, or we can follow the example of successful people in other fields of human endeavor and develop a dependable process for creating sales—and that's obviously the best and most rational approach to take.

—*Tom Morris, Philosopher and Author of "If Aristotle Ran General Motors"*

Contents

Acknowledgements

I had the privilege of being the youngest of six children in our family. I learned about life at the dinner table and about business from my father who was a paper salesman for more than fifty years. I listened to many conversations between him and my mother about how he would succeed and how she would manage in the meantime. I'm grateful to my father for teaching me how to put family first, customers a close second, and to run a business with both confidence and humility. I'm equally grateful to my mother for making it okay to ask questions.

A Philosophy and Pre-Med degree didn't prepare me for the career I chose. I have Holly and Dave Hanewall to thank for helping me shed the stigma of being a 'deep thinker that couldn't get into med school' and instead become an intern and full-time employee with IBM at a time when there was no chance of a guy with my education getting hired.

Many people helped me through my career at IBM, including my wife Tammy. We met, trained and even competed there, and she continues to teach me about business, love and life's blessings as we enjoy raising our two wonderful children (who continue to oblige me as I decide what I want to be when I grow up). Tom Bauer, Suzie Phillips, and Peter Brenner all had a lot to do with getting me moving at IBM (literally), and a long-time, long-distance friend of mine, Mike Scully, made me bleed blue and gain the knowledge, patience and confidence necessary to actually learn the sales trade.

Special thanks to my brother Craig for his confidence in me and allowing me to run my first business under his wing. It was the stepping stone to my most successful career, and I am grateful. Further, Craig helped me get through this project, and I never took it personally that he unleashed the 'frustrated editor' on me.

Thanks to Tom Slowey for plucking me out of an executive office suite, putting me behind the wheel of my most successful sales territory and catapulting me into my first management job. He brought me into a new industry, and made me part of a very special company full of fantastic people and experiences. A special thanks to Scott Steinbrecher, the grumpy old man who was my teacher, supporter and friend that made me far more successful than I could have been on my own. To my friends Flo, TJ, Terry Mahoney (and a bunch of others) … it was a great ride.

Tim Bradley quietly planted the seed that became this book. Tim continues to encourage me to share what I know, and will never stop teaching me more that I should include in works like this.

Thanks to Jeff Stiefler and Alan Gleicher, two businessmen that had the patience to teach and support a first-time CEO. They were instrumental in developing the company and turning my history of sales into an asset for operating all aspects of a business. To Lars, Mike and Geoff—thanks to each of you for pretty much the same thing.

And to everyone that I've worked with, beside and for that are not mentioned by name. I hope this book brings back some memories … what kind I will leave up to you …

Introduction

Very little of what you read here qualifies as 'original thought'. Even the title of this book is a phrase coined by a friend during our first consulting engagement.

But I've learned that 'original thought' is often less important than 'organization of thought'. In my early years with IBM, I went through training on how to maximize my time using an organizing 'system'. This 'system' was nothing more than a calendar, task list and address book all-in-one. I was told that the 'power' of the system was in its use as a 'single source of record'; a system I could use to plan, execute, prove and audit the steps I'd taken in executing my territory sales plan. That sounded much different than a standard calendar, task list and address book.

That's how you should think about this book: a system for *interrogating* your sales process and *improving* your results, and the *predictability* of your results, by making your process *repeatable*.

I've sold for many companies and built many sales teams. I've lead sales divisions and run companies. Each time I changed roles I essentially started over. I finally decided to organize the sales and management processes and sales tools I used effectively into a comprehensive, repeatable system. These pages distill years of observation, learning, training, attendance at sales seminars, development and use of selling collateral, and real-world experience into a step-by-step system for auditing a sales process.

How often have you heard the tired analogy comparing the sales organization to the "wild-west": a bunch of gunslingers on horseback, riding in hot pursuit of the speeding stagecoach, hoping to surprise the Expressmen and wrestle away the strong box? Put in terms of sales process: gunslingers (salespeople) each have their own horse and trail (sales process) for pursuing the coach. Expressmen (customers) must deliver their passengers (stockholders) to their destination (enterprise value). Regardless of the distance or hazards (getting lost, contracting disease, encountering wild animals or battling enemies), as long as the gunslinger returns with the strong box, the raid is considered a success.

To stretch the analogy, there are fewer stagecoaches today, Expressmen are smarter and better-equipped, and there are more lawmen (government regulations and corporate governance) to keep them from losing their strong box.

In the aftermath of modern-day accounting scandals, the idea that the stagecoach will be plundered without a well-designed plan is shortsighted. Like any other corporate function, the sales organization must interrogate its practices, and document its processes using 'Sarbanes-Oxley-like' rigor to 'comply' with the expectations of senior management by producing predictable results.

In the pages that follow, we'll explore the concept of the 'sales audit' and using it to achieve better predictability of results through 'sales process compliance'. We'll tie the audit to the expectations of senior management by answering these questions: How do executives view the current-state of sales team effectiveness? What skills do they believe are necessary to succeed in representing their product to the customer and winning business? Is the company hiring to these skills, tracking the skills through a defined sales process, and ultimately measuring the performance of the sales team on leveraging these skills in the execution of the sales plan?

Senior Executives and Sales Managers are ultimately after one thing: predictability in the ever-improving financial performance of the business. Business predictability has a direct impact on the perception of management's effectiveness, the dependability of the business' revenue stream, and ultimately enterprise value. The dependability of the revenue stream is the result of repeatable execution of a documented sales process, examination of the results, and modification of the process to assure future results. In a word, predictability depends on *regular audits* of the selling process.

The most unifying and necessary tool for a sales team is a documented and well-understood sales process. It creates a vocabulary for the entire team, sets expectations for the steps and timeframes of sale from qualification to closure, and level-sets the sales chain-of-command as to when to forecast revenue from a sales opportunity. Without a documented sales process, the sales organization is just a random band of gunslingers chasing random stagecoaches hoping to steal a strongbox. I've seen many sales processes, from the simple to the complex, and although different, they were not glaringly better or worse than the next.

What makes a sales process good-or-bad are results, and what most reliably achieves results is:

- A documented process, agreed-to and understood by the sales team
- A process that is followed by the sales team
- A process that yields predictable and consistent results
- A process that can be 'audited' for potential improvement

The primary purpose of performing a Sales Audit is to identify and document the existing sales process, uncover obstacles that hinder adoption and regular use of the process, measure the effectiveness of the process, and continually re-evaluate ways to improve the process to deliver results. The Enron scandal in the early

2000's fueled the advent of Sarbanes-Oxley legislation and the SOX Audit. CFOs, Controllers and anyone tied to financial measurement and reporting within a public company became very familiar with sections 302 and 404 of the legislation which introduced the requirement for audit and change controls around any process that impacted a company's financial results and reporting. Companies spent millions of dollars defining their processes, the control points around each process (who was involved at each touch-point or approval in the process), validating the segregation of duty at each control point (that the person requesting something cannot also approve the request), demonstrating the implementation and adoption of these processes, and auditing not only the consistent use of, but also any changes to, these processes in an effort to order to avoid someone manipulating the process for personal gain. The sales process (aside from the way the revenue was to be recognized by the company after the sale) largely avoided scrutiny because the process could vary so significantly due to human style and behavior. I contend that the sales process should undergo the same scrutiny-of-compliance through a Sales Audit as does the rest of the company under a SOX Audit.

Can the sales process be audited? Some sales managers would likely argue that selling is an art-form, a "rule-less" human process carried out by salespeople whose activities and styles vary with experience and tenure. They subscribe to the notion that as long as the sales organization produces results, there is no necessary process to be defined or audited.

I respect the view of the reader who considers selling to be an art. I can produce several examples of salespeople who produced significant results but followed no obvious process. However, there are far more examples of individuals who produce consistent, sustained results by following process in an 'artful' way. They use personal style as brushstrokes. They build trust and dialogue with decision-makers as they travel through a structured selling process. Art itself *is* a process. I argue that there would be no need for classes to teach sculpture, painting, or dance; form, genre or appreciation if this were not so. Without process training, all aspiring artists could reasonably be labeled 'masters'. It is my premise that the selling process is imbued with artistic interpretation, and the masterpiece is a finely crafted sale.

Consider the dangers of avoiding sales process audits. When economic times are good, the apparent ease of making sales calls evokes the old adage that "even turkeys can fly in a hurricane". But eventually the wind stops blowing and the turkeys come tumbling down. Having the forethought to audit, redefine and implement a sales process in advance of the dying wind is imperative for sustainable success.

The rigor of a customer's internal controls resulting from Sarbanes-Oxley has made the evaluation and justification of every investment more stringent. Evidence of thorough due-diligence and expected financial benefit is required before selecting a supplier. Once a selection is made, the process of actually procuring the solution is often new and unknown even to the user/buyer. This is particularly challenging for the sales team without a defined and well-understood process. It adds the complexity of getting the customer's money to the already complex task of convincing the customer to select their solution. Salespeople are required to be even more diligent in defining and executing the closing aspect of their selling process in order to deliver results as forecasted.

This book will walk us through the process of the Sales Audit together, explaining how to:

- Identify and articulate the gaps between the senior management's expectations of the sales team and those of the sales team itself.
- Interrogate the steps of the current sales process to evaluate its effectiveness at each step.
- Measure adherence to the process by the sales team and the results of the process.
- Review the performance of the process in terms of predictability of results
- Ensure the continual improvement of the process and its alignment with organizational results and expectations.

So let's begin the Sales Audit …

Chapter 1

Survey

Audit Point: Survey employees, throughout the company and in a cross-section of job functions, to identify company expectations and perceptions of the effectiveness of the sales process and team.

Control Document: Sales Audit Survey Document.

Following is the story of the birth of a sales process in a small company:

Executives (especially Founders and those that come up through the sales ranks), have strong opinions about how the product should be sold. They developed the presentations, delivered them to analysts, investors and customers, and have "pride-of-authorship". Executives have lived the company's story. Their history and authority make them extremely credible when delivering the company's message about its products. Their titles afford them a level of customer access normally unattainable by the typical salesperson. This access and credibility enhances their ability to effectively influence and make the sale. Executive 'batting averages' in final sales are high, and they may even be getting a 'hit with every trip to the plate'. With this high degree of success comes the executive's opinion that their presentations should be the standard for selling the company and its product.

(For established companies, please replace the word "executive" with any of the following and re-read the paragraph above: Marketing, Product Marketing, Sales Enablement, Sales Training or any other title responsible for taking the executive vision and turning it into collateral for delivery to the market).

Enter a new top sales executive, who, after being hired by the Executives or Founder, is provided the magic seeds of vision and product positioning (and the sales pitch to go along with them) from any of the above titled people. It is the new sales executive's job to plant these magic seeds within a sales process and to grow revenues. Through the trial-and-error of working with the sales people in the field, the top sales executive learns the messages that 'resonate' with potential customers, the contacts in the customer's organization who must be shown and convinced of the product's value, and what steps are necessary to justify the investment to complete a sale. The sales executive must then translate the resulting knowledge into a sales process that can be supported by senior management, communicated to the sales team and deeply established as standard operating procedure against which all salespeople will be measured.

Time passes and the pressure of meeting quotas intensifies. The value of implementing a well-defined sales process is blurred by senior management's shifting focus to sales results. The company has needs, and senior executives are less concerned with *how* the product is being sold than with ***how much*** is being sold. The inevitable happens ...

Before the top sales executive has implemented a well-defined process, before it is communicated and the sales team is educated, before collateral can be developed from what was learned in the field, before sales people have been evaluated for their effectiveness, revenue expectations demand that the sales team be expanded. To shorten the ramp to increased revenue, the top sales executive is expected to hire people who "already know how to sell" and to just let them "go forth and multiply". The company message is taught to new-hires in 'shotgun' style: during ride-along training or week-long binge-drinking boot camps where new salespeople are expected to "get the hang of it". The expanded team hits the field for some trial-and-error selling using the message and whatever they 'typically do' in a sales process. Now there are more salespeople with no defined or consistent process, and the message continues to morph as the salespeople alter it to deliver on their only objective: sales results.

Over time, each salesperson 'individualizes' the sales process and the message. With divergent processes come divergent results, and only a few salespeople who serendipitously use the right process and deliver the right message with any given prospect will succeed. The rest fail. Those that fail, leave, only to be replaced with others who start the cycle all over again. Eventually the sales team has high turnover, and revenues begin to retreat. The top sales executive wakes up one morning after reporting that sales results are down and asks "What happened"?

The top sales executive knows that there are too many variables in a selling process that has no defined structure; that he has few, if any, salespeople that have the necessary skills and are aligned with the company's message; and there are no metrics in place to explain the poor results. Unable to convince company executives that the results would have met expectation had they allowed him to install the system he had developed from the sales audit, the top sales executive resigns.

The End.

This is when companies will finally consider a Sales Audit to interrogate their sales process, and yet it is arguably the very worst time. One of my favorite T.V. commercials was from EDS and aired during the big football game in January, 2000:

Fade in: the sky is grey, and a man in a hardhat is yelling over the wind. He is extolling the virtues of his job and how much he enjoys building complex airplanes and putting them in the air.

The camera pans back: the man in a hardhat is shown to be working on the wing of an aircraft that is half-built, incomplete, but already in flight.

A second commercial by the same company:

Fade in: the sky is deep blue. A cowboy on horseback with a western twang is sharing his love for the job of "bringing in the herd".

The camera pans back: the cowboy, instead of driving cattle, is herding thousands of cats who are roaming the range.

Waiting until the sales process fails, then having to modify the process while you're trying to improve results is akin to building a plane while it's flying. Working with individualized sales processes and individualized messages is akin to herding cats. The answer would have been to implement the solutions identified by the sales audit when sales were up-and-to-the-right in order to allow adjustments to be made without panic. Although there is never a good time to do an audit, a company must do one, implement the process defined from it, and then do audits *regularly* and implement the resulting changes to the sales process *iteratively*.

A sales audit is initiated through surveys beginning at the senior executive level. The highest ranking officers in the company define measures of success. There are usually no hard-and-fast rules that sales must follow in the sales process, only revenue expectations set by senior executives against which every salesperson is judged. These same executives will have strong opinions on the sales message as well as how they perceive the sales process could be improved. Surveying for those expectations and opinions starts at the top:

Executive Management	CEO
	CFO
	COO
	EVP
	HR

The rest of the company has expectations for the way the product should be represented to the potential customer. Like the executives, other stakeholders in the company's success will have strong opinions on the sales message (if not the process itself). It is these people who witness the various deliveries of the message and observe various subtleties in the selling process. They work with customers closely to determine their reactions during and after the selling process, and hear how satisfied the customer was with the process as they support product installation and are expected to deliver the value promised. *Surveys must include the non-executive sales-related teams*, responsible for the day-to-day task of supporting the implementation of the product. Some of the titles to be included in surveying:

Sales Management	**Direct Sales (Outside and Inside)**
	Indirect/Channel Sales
Sales	**Top Performers**
	New-Hires
	Poor Performers
Sales Support	
Services	
Product Marketing	

Although each conversation is unique, the basic premise of surveying is to derive individual feedback (unbiased and confidential) while identifying common opinions on the way selling *should be done* (expectations) and the way it *actually is done* (current state).

The following sample questions should be provided in advance to those being surveyed, in hopes of crystallizing thought prior to the survey and streamlining the process of conducting the survey:

1. Describe your sales team's performance (separate from quota attainment)
2. What are your Sales Team's Top 3 Strong/Weak characteristics?
3. Give me your elevator pitch …
4. Describe the sales process as you understand it.
5. Which of the steps are most often missed in the sales process?
6. What skills are most critical for sales success?
7. Have you hired to these skills? Why or why not?

8. How would you describe the sales training process? How would you change it?
9. Which sales tools do you think are most consistently used? Which ones are effective?
10. Are there any sales tools missing from the sales kit?
11. Are salespeople held accountable for execution of a defined sales process? Are they held accountable for results? How would you suggest this be changed?

Exhibit A is a sample of an actual Sales Audit Survey Document used during a previous sales audit. Although each survey document will vary by company, a survey document must be developed and used in order to ensure completeness and consistency of the information gathered. Take some time to familiarize yourself with the survey document and you will begin to see how the survey can draw-out the opinions of the sales process held by stakeholders in the company.

Sales Audit Survey Document

	CEO	Executives	Sales Executives	Sales Reps
Rate the Sales Team's Overall Effectiveness (aside from quota attainment)				
Sales #1 Strength				
Sales #1 Weakness				
Recruiting				
How well have you defined repeatable skills?				
How well have you defined the interview process?				
Training				
How long before a rep should be productive?				
Which tools are used religiously? Which tools are not used and why?				
Company Positioning				
How do customer/prospects perceive your company?				
When the Rep leaves, what impression should be left with the customer?				
How in synch are marketing and field operations?				
How consistent should messaging be (vs. stylistic)?				
Elevator Pitch				
The CBI (Critical Business Issue)				
The Value Proposition				
The Company (Who we are. What we do. How well we do it)				
The References				
The Space				
The Competition				
Lead Generation and Relationships				
Effectiveness of Trade Shows				
Telesales Scripted?				
What % of leads passed are truly qualified? At what levels)?				
How important is building rapport? At what levels)?				
How effectively do Reps Build/Keep Relationships (Influencers, Technical Buyers, Coaches)?				
How effectively do Reps Build/Keep Executive Relationships (Equal Business Stature)?				
Product Positioning and Justification				
How well are the Value Propositions defined?				
How well are requirements documented and addressed (technical and business)?				
What percentage of the sale is related to issues of technology? business?				
To Whom is the Product most effectively sold?				
How well do Reps sell to ROI?				

Exhibit A—Sales Audit Survey Document

Sales Process

Is the sales process documented and understood at all levels?											
Your understanding of the process steps?											
How are salespeople held accountable for meeting criteria at each step?											
Where do most deals stall?											
What tools exist at each stage of the selling process? What tools are missing?											
Are you confident that reps effectively run sales calls? (5P's)											
What are your expectations on sales cycle timeframes?											
What are some typical Rep pitfalls?											
How well do Reps handle objections											
What are some of the typical objections?											
Can the Reps whiteboard as well as they PowerPoint?											
How well do the Reps know their competition?											
How is the quality of an opportunity measured?											
How effectively do Reps handle multiple opportunities (Territory Management)?											
How much revenue is the result of new business vs. follow-on business?											

Pricing

What are the Company's expectations with regard to deal size?											
How well do Reps handle negotiation?											
How much freedom is given to negotiate?											
How complicated is the pricing structure?											
Where is your Company priced with regard to the Market?											

Resources

When should the Rep involve Company Executives in the sale (and when shouldn't they)?											
What key resources are at the Reps disposal?											
Are the resources used sparingly and as a negotiation technique?											

Predictability and Forecasting

How accurate is the forecast?											
Why isn't the forecast more accurate (are Reps chasing ghosts)?											
What kind of visibility into the forecast do you have?											
What should the percent-to-close be?											
What other metrics should be used to measure sales progress?											
What information do you need to be better educated?											

Deliverables

What percentage of your business starts as an RFI?											
How consistent are proposals? RFI responses?											

Review Process

How well do Reps recognize their own strengths/weaknesses?											
How formal and regular are your reviews? How long is a rep allowed to underperform?											
How well are the compensation plans structured to meet company objectives?											

Exhibit A—Sales Audit Survey Document (cont'd)

The following pages show actual survey results from a previous sales audit conducted in an $80 million software company. Take some time to familiarize yourself with the survey results. Although these are the deliverables from the Sales Audit Survey Document, you get a distinct feel for the opinions of those surveyed. These opinions are then categorized into: *trends* (common opinions amongst those surveyed) and *gaps* (either disparate opinions amongst those surveyed, or wide differences between the expectations of those surveyed and what is actually happening in the field). Trends and gaps form the foundation of the improvements to make in the sales process in order to meet expectations.

Sales Audit Survey Results

Executive Summary

Objective:

Interview a cross-section of company executives, sales and marketing employees. Identify gaps in existing sales messaging and process.

Employees Surveyed:

Executive Management:	CFO
	EVP Worldwide Ops
	Senior Director, International Operations
Sales Management:	Area Vice President, Channels
	Area Vice President, South
	Area Vice President, West
	Area Vice President, East
	Managing Director EMEA
	Manager, Financial Services
National Account Managers:	Northeast
	Southeast
	Central
	West
Pre-Sales Consultants:	Northeast
	Southeast
	Central
	West
Product Marketing:	Manager

Current State: Sales Process and Training

The Company has selected and delivered a 3rd Party sales methodology and training to the field. Since the initial training, no reinforcement training has been delivered, and management has not unanimously adopted or mandated the use of the methodology and tools.

Corporate sponsored sales training is limited to technology updates upon changes to the product offering or message re-positioning as deemed necessary by product marketing. Since abolishing the sales training team and sales 'boot camp', in-field training is either non-existent or entirely ad hoc as determined by local management.

Upon hiring new sales personnel, or quarterly upon an informal assessment of team skills, local management requests corporate resources to deliver one-off training sessions. Although the necessary topics appear to have some consistency across geographies, the requests are not aggregated and training schedules and agendas are not synchronized.

Ad Hoc training sessions on sales process typically consist of a 'parade of personnel' delivering lectures, often extemporaneously with formats ranging from PowerPoint presentations, to 'chalk talks', to roundtables. Training material quality ranges from all-inclusive binders to no deliverables at all. Presenters vary and often fail to adequately prepare for the sessions, further exacerbating the inconsistency of topics, materials, quality of delivery and replication of results. Sessions do not routinely include reinforcement exercises or testing to 'internalize' learning.

Technical training for Pre-Sales Consultants is delivered uniquely by geography (domestic v. international), but both consist of predominantly public (customer fee-based) courses. The U.S. requires a two-day course, while International requires Pre-Sales Consultants to attend additional courses typically reserved for Professional Services Consultants and deep-product certification. International personnel believe that International customers are significantly more sophisticated and require the additional training. They also believe that joint training sessions are impractical as a result. In-field training is typically dependent upon technology releases or ad hoc as determined by Pre-Sales management.

Current State: Sales Tools and Resources

A number of tools and resources delivered by corporate were identified for use by sales personnel throughout the selling process. The list below is not definitive, but is evidence that the company is extremely responsive to sales' request for in-field support. Some of the tools on the list have been 'graded' base on the consistency of use and effectiveness when implemented (those without 'grades' were tools receiving mention by only a few interviewees):

	Consistent	Effective
Tools:		
Best Practice Sales Process (9-Steps) Laminated Card	A	C
Solution Map/Interactive Solution Map	A	B
Competitive Playbooks		
Combat Kit		
Benchmark Certification Questions	D	B
Presentations:		
Chalk talk	D	C
EPP Presentation (replacing CPM Positioning Presentation)		
Hook Presentation	C	C
Pre-Sales Engineer Video Presentations		
CIO Presentation		
Systems:		
Solution Library (Survey Data & Blueprints)		
CRM	D	D
Document Repository	B	D
Forecasting		
Resources:		
Visibility Assessment	D	C
Proof of Concept; Fast-Start Templates/Models		
Client Reference Process/Quarterly Reference Roundtable	B	A
Advisory Board		
Accelerated Results Methodology (ARM)		
VMA Telemarketing	B	D
Whitepaper: Selling against Spreadsheets		
Executive Sponsors		

Partnerships:
Analyst Positioning Reports
Partnership Meetings   A   D

Events:
Executive Briefing
Quarterly In-Region Marketing Briefings
Best Practices Lab Planning Session

As indicated by 'grade', the challenge of the company in the Sales Audit Survey Results above is managing the sheer number of tools (quality, ease of access, content currency and ownership) and how consistently the field uses them ('right tool for the right job': effectiveness of the tool and appropriateness within given steps of the selling cycle).

As you read through the results, you likely noticed that the opinions resulting from the surveys can be categorized as follows:

Trends:

> Standard sales methodology
> Company is responsive to request for sales tools and deliverables

Gaps:

> Lack of consistent or standard in-field training
> Number of sales tools is overwhelming; under-used and ineffective

The primary result of the surveys is to gather expectations and opinions about the sales process. These opinions are categorized to reveal trends and gaps, which then become areas of focus for improvement. In our example, training and sales tools would be a primary focus as we continue the Sales Audit.

The Sales Audit continues by interrogating each aspect of the Sales Audit Survey Document (recruiting, training, the sales process and the sales performance review). The subsequent chapters in this book will explore ways to leverage the trends and gaps revealed through surveying into improvements in the sales process and selling results.

So let's explore ways to leverage survey results to improve the second step of the Sales Audit: recruiting sales talent to the company.

Chapter 2

Using Survey Results to Recruit Sales Talent

Audit Point: The interview process must test sales candidates for the presence of the skills identified as critical to success through the Sales Audit Survey.

Control Document: Sales Interview Form and Profile Test.

Now … this is going to feel like I'm either taking you on a detour, or I've driven off the road altogether. You're likely asking yourself "what has recruiting got to do with auditing the sales process"? Well, *a complete sales audit interrogates all components of the sales process, and successful execution of the sales process begins with recruiting talent capable of following a process and getting results.* One of the early concepts I learned at IBM was the GIGO concept: Garbage In, Garbage Out. No matter how good the computer program was, if you filled it with lousy data you got lousy results. The Sales Audit will reveal the same: if you have lousy salespeople following even a great sales process, you'll get lousy results.

Chapter One demonstrated that the first step in a Sales Audit is utilizing surveys to reveal a gap between expectations and reality. Many of the questions in the Sales Audit Survey target the activities, behaviors, knowledge and skills of the sales team. The results of the survey (trends that show skills overwhelmingly present or gaps that show expected skills overwhelmingly absent from the sales team) define the skills the company expects and requires of successful sales employees. Once these critical skills are defined, they are built into the hiring criteria; questions are designed to identify these traits and test for the presence of these skills in employment candidates.

Let's look at an example. Below I've pulled some of the questions from the Sales Audit Survey document. Notice that many of the questions used in audit interviews deal with sales activity and behavior:

Sales' #1 Strength
Sales' #1 Weakness
The CBI (Critical Business Issue)
The Value Proposition
The Company (Who we are, What we do, How well we do it)?
How effectively do Reps Build/Keep Executive Relationships?
How well do Reps sell to ROI?
Are you confident that reps effectively run sales calls?
How well do reps handle objections?
How well do the Reps know their competition?
How well do Reps handle negotiation?
Why is/isn't the forecast more accurate (are Reps chasing ghosts)?

Let's assume that the majority of the survey respondents overwhelmingly agreed that 'Sales #1 Strength' is their intense commitment to the company. Let's also assume that the majority of the survey respondents overwhelmingly agreed that the salespeople should be able to deliver 'The Value Proposition' clearly to prospects but aren't doing so. Now categorize these trends and gaps into sales skills that are deemed critical to sales success in the company:

1) Commitment to the Company
2) Translating Value

In order to ensure that future sales employees possess these 'critical skills', sales management must include the categories in the employment interview process and develop interview questions to test for the presence of these 'critical skills'.

Exhibit B is an example of a Sales Interview Form resulting from surveys during a previous sales audit. The critical skills fell into 11 categories broken into two groups: Performance Skills and General Skills. Also included are examples of at least two different questions that were developed to test for the presence of the General Skills during interviews.

Take some time to familiarize yourself with the Sales Interview Form and associated questions.

Candidate: _____

Interviewer: _____
Interview Date: _____

Skill Strength

Strong ←————→ Weak

Performance Skills:

Comments:

History of Performance Against Quota
Sales Process Execution
Tools Utilization
Pipeline Growth
Accuracy of Forecasting

General Selling Skills:

Accountability
Ability to Convey Value to Customer
Perceptive to Customer Needs
Verbal and Written Communications
Decision Making and Problem Solving
Recognition and Handling of Objections
Juggling Tasks and Managing Chaos

Total Overall Rating:

Recommendation: Hire _____ Not Hire _____

Reasons for Recommendation: _____
_____

Exhibit B—Interview Form, page 1

Accountability

Q. Give me any specific examples of times when you found it necessary to give long hours to your job.

A.

Q. Tell me about a time when you were able to provide your own motivation even though you were working alone. What were the circumstances and how did you manage to motivate yourself?

A.

Ability to Convey Value to Customer

Q. Solutions can often involve a 'language' specific to the company but unfamiliar to a customer. Tell me about a time when you were able to translate the benefits of a solution into something meaningful to the customer.

A.

Q. Tell me about the last time you were able to win a deal even though your solution was inferior to the competition.

A.

Perceptive to Customer Needs

Q. It is sometimes difficult to perceive a customer's needs. Tell me about a time when you were able to think like a customer in order to discover his or her unique perspective.

A.

Q. Tell me how your knowledge of personality differences benefitted your effectiveness with a customer.

A.

Verbal and Written Communications

Q. Tell me about a specific experience of yours that illustrates your ability to ask intelligent questions and gain knowledge critical to a sale.

A.

Q. Give an example of a time when you were able to build rapport with a customer even though the situation was a difficult one.

A.

Exhibit B—Interview Form, page 2

Decision Making and Problem Solving

Q. In many problem situations, it is tempting to jump to conclusions and quickly build a solution. Tell me about a time when you resisted this temptation and gathered all the facts associated with a problem before coming to a solution.

A.

Q. Describe in detail a situation with an angry customer in which you made a decision which required sound judgement.

A.

Recognition and Handling of Objections

Q. Most organizations have a political environment which impacts the way you get things done. Tell me about a time when you worked within the system, handling a political situation effectively.

A.

Q. Give me an example of when you were able to manipulate the poser/influence system to close a sale.

A.

Juggling Tasks and Managing Chaos

Q. Sometimes it is necessary to work in unsettled or rapidly-changing circumstances. When have you found yourself in that position? What exactly did you do?

A.

Q. Tell me about a time when you were successful working in an unstructured work environment.

A.

Exhibit B—Interview Form, page 2 (cont'd)

The hiring process in some companies is a bit 'loosey-goosey', while it is a militaristic trip through regimented terror in others. Your company must decide who is included in the interview process, how many people need to 'fingerprint the suspect', and whether it's done in a dark room under a bright light or informally on the golf course. I've participated in many types, and your company's personality should dictate the participants and the venue for interviewing. However, the candidate <u>and</u> the company want at least three things from the interview process:

1) To demonstrate that the company has a defined and thorough process.
2) That the company has conducted an impressive and enlightening interview.
3) That the information exchanged is meaningful to both parties and will result in the best decision.

I've been involved in numerous interviews that violated one or more of the above. One interview was forty-minutes long, with thirty-eight minutes spent discussing the Catholic Church (and the candidate wasn't even catholic). So, as impersonal or unconventional as it may seem, use the Sales Interview Form religiously (no pun intended) to ensure better results.

In order to effectively use the Sales Interview Form, there is one thing you must do in order to avoid having a candidate clam-up or pass-out during such a structured interview: explain the document and its virtues to the candidate prior to beginning the interview. Perhaps a statement like this:

"We've surveyed the company as part of a Sales Audit and have found the following skill sets to be important to success with our company: [read the categories to the candidate here]. We've developed questions that we ask of each candidate to validate whether or not they have these skills. Our interview may seem a bit more structured than you're used to, but we want to make certain that you have the skills required to succeed at this company and in this position". [Now, put the form on the table, out in the open, and actually read one of the questions from each category. Write bullet points from the candidate's answers next to the questions. Once the interview is over and the candidate leaves, summarize your bullet points by indicating the presence of the skill (or lack thereof) with a check in the appropriate box on page one of the form].

At first the candidate may be thrown off. But soon enough (maybe not until after the candidate leaves) they will recognize and appreciate that the company is well-prepared, has a consistent method for interviewing, judges all candidates fairly against the needs of the job and cares about their ability to succeed. Using the document shows that the company has conducted a fair and impartial interview. It also serves as a well-documented audit trail for substantiating the decision to hire or pass on a candidate. It can even serve as a source of information after-the-fact as to why a person that was hired actually succeeded or failed at the company.

The company has carried out a successful interview and has a candidate or two considered for hire because they have demonstrated the skills determined to be critical to succeeding at the company. Several interviews may have been conducted with each of the candidates. But don't unqualified, 'professional interviewees' still slip through this process? Sometimes, yes. So I suggest one more test to validate that the company hasn't stumbled on a 'professional interviewee' instead of a truly qualified candidate: a Behavioral Profile.

The Behavioral Profile asks a series of questions that map behavior back to the skills deemed critical to the job. There are many third-party companies that offer the service of customizing profile test questions and putting the test (and results) online. The behavioral profile helps weed-out 'professional interviewees' who may have slipped through the interview process because the skills are validated through questions too obsequious for the interviewee to anticipate. Further, the test asks questions in a multitude of scenarios, restates the same question in different ways, and tests for presence of a skill several times. Only a consistent response reveals whether or not a particular skill actually exists in the candidate, and it is nearly impossible for a candidate to mentally track consistency of their responses.

Think of it like this: your candidate approaches a blackjack table and attempts to count cards to win. The candidate may be able to count cards in a single deck, but when the dealer has a shoe filled with five decks, the task of counting (and winning) is nearly impossible. When your candidate attempts to spot the skill in this behavioral profile test, it will be impossible to consistently 'manufacture a response' and consistently 'fool' the results. The Behavior Profile is an objective way to validate the skills of a candidate.

Further, the profile test can and should be used when charting the results of the reference check(s) performed about the candidate. Many companies forego the reference check (in lieu of "insiders" or people in the "network" that know the candidate). Bad idea. In fact, a company should check each of the references provided by the candidate (I usually ask for a subordinate, a peer, a manager and a customer that worked with the candidate). You might also find someone that knows the candidate that was *not* a reference provided. The extra effort will be worth it.

Background checks are also imperative. As a CEO, I was interviewing for a CIO to join our organization. The candidate was probably one of the best "actors" I've ever encountered, having gotten by me and the executive team in the interviews. When performing the reference check, he passed with flying colors. When performing the background check, one of the jobs he cited on his resume didn't line up with the time he indicated he was employed. When we contacted the employer, it turned out that he had been a contractor with the company, not an employee as the candidate had represented. Further, a letter of recommendation the candidate had submitted from the same company turned out to be a fake (logos and signatures taken from a document on the internet). Needless to say, we didn't hire the candidate … but he and I had a nice chat …

Exhibit C is an example of how I'd like to see the results from a behavior profile test. Note that the categories against which the candidate's skills are charted should follow the categories identified in the Sales Interview document.

Behavioral Profile

Match to Company Expectation

	10	9	8	7	6	5	4	3	2	1	
Committed to Task			R		X						Not Committed to Task
Able to Translate Value				X		R					Unable to Translate Value
Perceptive			X	R	R						Not Perceptive
Command of Spoken Communications				R		X					No Command of Spoken Communications
Able to Make Decisions					XR						Unable to Make Decisions
Reads the System						X	R				Does Not Read the System
Tolerates of Ambiguity			X		R						Intolerant of Ambiguity
Background Check Clean	X										Background Check Not Clean

Key:

	Company Average/Expectation
X	Behavioral Profile Result of Candidate
R	Reference Check Average Result

Exhibit C—Behavior Profile Results (Adapted from Corporate Psychology Resources/Talent Quest)

The company *finally* has as complete a picture as it can have about a potential candidate's match to the skills deemed critical to succeed as part of the sales team.

Through the Sales Audit Survey, trends and gaps are identified in sales skills and categorized into 'critical skill types'. The Sales Audit process ensures that the company is testing for these skills in the employment interviews, and using a Behavioral Profile Test, reference check and background check to validate that the candidate 'behaves' consistently with the skills (and isn't just a smooth talker). This should help eliminate the 'garbage' variable in the GIGO problem and put more qualified sales people in the field to execute on a sales process.

Recruitment of better sales talent is clearly important if you are starting from scratch. However, most companies already have a well-established sales team that they are complementing through recruitment. How do we use the Sales Audit to ensure that the company's process accounts for evaluating whether some of the existing team may need to be upgraded? In Chapter Twelve we'll discuss the Performance Review Process, and you'll note striking similarities and extreme consistency in how a company should evaluate new sales talent and re-evaluate existing sales team members.

With better sales talent, is sales management ready to focus the Sales Audit on the efficiency of the sales process itself? Not yet …

Chapter 3

Using Survey Results to Train Sales Talent

Audit Point: The training process must develop and/or reinforce the skills expected of a salesperson.

Control Document: Sales Training Syllabus

Hiring correctly doesn't completely eliminate the GIGO problem.

Training is as important as hiring for the following reason: how many times has the perfect candidate been hired and been entirely prepared to represent the company in the field? *Never.* How many times has the perfect candidate been hired and sales management has *assumed* they were entirely prepared to represent the company in the field? *Every time.* The typical hiring manager often thinks the job is complete when the candidate is hired. "Sink or swim I always say". Well, we'll need a bit more preparation than is typical to minimize GIGO and improve the new salesperson's chance for success. *A Sales Audit will reveal whether sales management has an appropriate training program for preparing new-hires to be successful in the field.*

That first day is an important indicator for the new employee. They'll be trying to validate that what they were told during the interview process about the company is true. They'll be evaluating whether they've joined a successful, well-managed company that is concerned about their success. Right about now, some readers are rolling their eyes and murmuring "talented sales people (if, indeed, that's what we're getting from the results of our Sales Audit of the hiring process in chapters one and two), don't need a bunch of care-and-feeding. In fact, most really good sales people don't want to leave the field for training at all. Just unleash 'em and let 'em go". Well, sales management needs to deliver training if for no other reason than to continue to demonstrate that the company is serious about the skills required to be successful, about finding the right talent, and about enabling that talent to deliver on expected sales results.

There's another reason sales management needs to have training plans in order: it's likely that there have been '*trade-offs*' made somewhere in the hiring process (i.e., the employee has some skills, but not all the skills that sales management is looking for). Every new salesperson will need to develop certain knowledge and/or skills (i.e., product knowledge) or simply will need reinforcement and 'tweaking' of pre-existing skills (i.e., translating business value for a new solution). If sales management is to get the results they expect, they'll need to make sure that the skills they were looking for in the interview process are enhanced and developed in order to get the results the candidate (and the company) needs.

This sounds pretty detailed, and suggests that we're about to develop a full training curriculum before moving on. Not so. The skills have already been identified in the Sales Audit Survey, and in the same way those skills were built into the interviewing process, so must they be built into the training regimen.

Exhibit D is an example of a potential five-week training regimen based on the Sales Audit Survey and Sales Interview Form we've discussed in prior chapters. Take some time to familiarize yourself with the Sales Training Syllabus.

	WK 1	WK 2	WK 3	WK 4	WK 5
Introduction to the Company					
New Employee Training	16.0				
Meet the Senior Leadership Team					
- CEO (Values, Vision and Company Development)		0.5			
- CFO (Financial Stability and Strength)		0.5			
- COO (Product Development, Company Objectives)		0.5			
- SVP, HR (Expectations, Organization)	1.0				
- SVP, Marketing (Product Positioning)		1.0			
The Business Problem					
Reading: Trade Journals					
Sales Process Books		After Hours			
Marketing Presentations					
Company Positioning					
Company Sales Presentation and Certification		8.0	8.0		
Chalk Talk			8.0		
Demonstration and Certification					8.0
The Elevator Pitch					
The CBI	8.0				
The Value Proposition	8.0				
The References			8.0		
The "Space" and Market				8.0	
The Competition				8.0	
Common Objection Handling				8.0	
Situational Role Plays (Qualifying, Sales Calls, Competition)					8.0
Lead Generation and Relationships					
Qualification Flowchart and Lead passing Process		2.0			
Building Relationships with the Right People					2.0
Product Positioning and Justification					
Navigating your Accounts			2.0		
Review Sales Kit				2.0	
Running the Sales Call (the 5Ps)				2.0	
When to engage Resources				2.0	
How Customers Allocate Budget				2.0	
On-line Product Information and Brochure Review			2.0		
Review the ROI Model			2.0		
Review Case Study Library			2.0		
Sales Process					
Territory Definition			2.0		
Building a Business Plan				6.0	
Pre-Sales Activity					2.0
The TenStep Sales Process					2.0
Building Strategy					2.0
Proving Value					2.0
Managing the Pipeline					2.0
The Customer Approval Process					2.0
Contracts and Negotiation					2.0
In-Field Training					
Listening-In (On-the-Phones) with Inside Sales		2.0			
Product Demonstrations with Product Marketing and Support		4.0			
Ride-Alongs (Shadowing) with Top Salesperson		16.0			
Pricing					
Price Book Review and Exercises			2.0	2.0	2.0
Predictability and Forecasting					
Compensation Plan					2.0
Activity Plans and Executive Letters					2.0
Forecasting Methodology and CRM System					2.0
Total for Week	33.0	34.5	36.0	40.0	40.0

Exhibit D—Sales Training Syllabus

Note that the training categories match those of the Sales Audit Survey document in **Exhibit A**. A similarly detailed syllabus and the underlying materials must be given to the new sales employee.

Specific elements of each training syllabus will vary based on the company's sales model, industry, and maturity that the sales process demands. Note in **Exhibit D** that there is a section dedicated to executive exposure and in-field exposure to sales peers in the first two weeks. This time will afford the new salesperson an opportunity to prepare for executive and customer meetings, build credibility and a relationship with the executive team and their peers, better internalize executive expectations and in-field messaging early-on, and allow their executives and teammates to get a snapshot of the new salesperson's current-state of readiness for the field. Although seemingly early in the new salesperson's career with the company, these sessions serve as a 'check-and-balance' on salespeople that make it past the interviewing process and into the company culture.

The Sales Audit examines current company processes to ensure that sales talent will succeed as a result of a skills-based selection process and training program. The Sales Audit will likely result in modifying the hiring and training process to one that is more costly now than in the past, and this will necessarily elevate the expectations of management. So now is the time to point the Sales Audit at the process salespeople are following in the field to ensure we meet management expectations and deliver results.

Chapter 4

The Selling Cycle

Audit Point: The Selling Cycle documents the steps, associated tasks and appropriate tools for closing sales opportunities within a territory. Progress must be measurable at each step.

Control Document: The Selling Cycle.

The Sales Audit begins with the surveying of all stakeholders in the sales process to understand expectations and identify trends/gaps between the expectations and reality. Survey results fortify the hiring and training processes to ensure that newly-hired employees have a better opportunity to succeed out of the gate. Once the surveying and interview processes are established, the focus of the Sales Audit turns to the issue of defining a repeatable process for managing customers and sales opportunities in the field.

Although every company's sales process is unique based on the company's approach to the market, the targeted buyer and countless other factors, it is safe to say that all sales processes will have certain steps that are similar. **Exhibit E** is a graphical representation of what we will term the Selling Cycle:

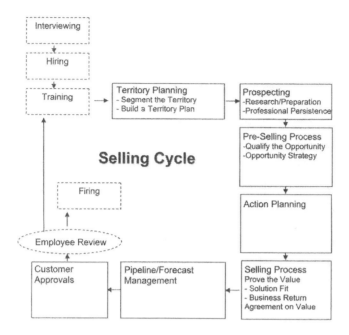

Exhibit E—The Selling Cycle

The Selling Cycle should be a way to ensure that the sales team has an understanding of the sales process step-by-step, and that the tools and tasks associated with each step are identified, developed, available and explained to the sales team. The Selling Cycle should be modular so that the company is able to continually improve on each specific step in the process. This way, problem modules can be isolated, identified and fixed without disruption to those steps that are working well. This keeps the sales team moving forward while allowing the sales manager to iteratively introduce change to the process, tools, hiring and training.

The Sales Audit continues in subsequent chapters, as we walk through an analysis of each step in this cycle, examining the process, tools and training that are necessary at each step in order to ensure overall cycle success.

Chapter 5

Territory Planning: Segment the Territory

Audit Point:　　　　　Sales Management must segment sales territories in order to focus their salespeople on accounts that demonstrate a need for their solution. This should start with targeting accounts that fit the company's initial business plan and/or are most like the company's profitable customers.

Control Document:　　Territory Segmentation Filters.

Indulge me for a couple of pages. The concepts you'll read in the following pages are ridiculously obvious. But the purpose of the Sales Audit is to revisit company processes, and *revisiting the company's process for territory segmentation will have an impact on the sales team's productivity and the company's success.*

Sales Management typically divides territories by geography: U.S. broken into areas, areas into regions, regions into districts, and districts into territories. Mature companies may remove vertical markets, or isolate large accounts from mid-size and small accounts. They may even choose to segment territories with an existing customer base from one that is purely for prospecting new accounts. Young companies may include all vertical markets, strategic and mid-size accounts, customers and prospects all in an alphabetical list as they continue to refine the market they serve. Regardless of company maturity or management decisions, the job of sales management remains the same: segment territories for the salespeople so that they quickly identify specific targets in the territory that have a need for the solution. Unfortunately, sales management tends to shortcut the segmentation process, and territories are often determined like this:

The sales manager assigns a county, city, series of zip codes or area codes to Salesperson (A), who pulls (off of some marketing database) an alphabetized list of accounts within the geography they've been given and attacks over the phone moving from A to Z. When they find an opportunity it goes up on their board, and they move to the next letter of the alphabet. What naturally occurs is that the salesperson identifies fifteen-to-twenty opportunities before they hit the letter 'M'. Their sales manager holds a regular territory review and concludes that there's plenty of opportunity in the alphabetized territory list, and that the salesperson is now out-of-bandwidth (has no time to prospect for new opportunities). The manager decides that the territory is big enough to add another salesperson, and Salesperson (A) becomes the "A—M Territory Representative" and a new salesperson (Salesperson (B)) is hired to be the "N—Z Territory Representative". Now, this isn't necessarily a bad thing, as improved performance comes with territory focus (I'm a huge fan of focus and removing the 'noise' that most salespeople can become embroiled in). But the challenge is that Salesperson (A) is now backed into a corner. Example: what if, in this 'A—M Territory', all of the accounts are the small businesses that wanted to be first in the phonebook (AAA Roto-Rooter, ACME Blowtorch Repair), and those recognizable-brand accounts are in the 'N—Z Territory' (Wells Fargo Bank and Zurich Insurance)? Although Salesperson (A) currently has identified opportunities, the yield could likely be a bunch of small transactions, while Salesperson (B) has all of the bigger strategic accounts to prospect and sell.

All new salespeople want a quick-start. Their managers want them to start fast too. The quickest way to get going in a territory is not to just pick-up the phone and start calling. Rather it is to match the territory list back to the company's customer definition. The salesperson interprets this as looking for certain qualifiers such as 'companies with revenues greater than X' or 'companies with more than Y number of employees', and will turn to information sources (OneSource, Local Business Journals, SIC Code Listings, Hoover's/D&B, etc.). The salesperson ends-up with a complete list of companies in their geography sorted by qualifier (revenue, number of employees, or some other measure of opportunity that has little to do with the company's best prospects), and if the salesperson is uncertain as to the company's clear market definition, virtually *every company in their list becomes a prospect.* When everyone is a prospect, ***what starts out as a salesperson selling a product into a market, turns into the salesperson trying to define the market for selling a product.*** Insurance salespeople sell this way every day: the product has inherent value to everyone, but it is difficult to sell the product based on need since the customer is not sure how long it will be before they actually have a need for, or will derive benefit from, the product.

Sales Management must help the salesperson match a territory list back to a company's market definition to identify prospects that have the need for the company's offering rather than just the desire or potential to use it. ***When segmenting a territory list, sales management should work with the salesperson to identify those companies that:***

1. *Serve markets similar to customers that have already purchased the solution*
2. *Are capable of spending money of this magnitude on vendor solutions*
3. *Will be a recognizable and credible reference once successful with the solution*

This is easier said than done, as the company may be new, or have a new product that has just entered the market, and no reference base exists. Let's look at three different company scenarios where the approach to segmentation will differ:

1) Prospecting for the Company's First Customers
2) Prospecting for Follow-On Customers
3) Prospecting for Follow-On Product Opportunities with Existing Customers

Prospecting for the Company's First Customers: If the organization is too new to have an established client base, segmentation is even more critical in order to land those first cornerstone clients. Sales Management must make certain that the salespeople stay true to the original message, and test the markets as defined in the original business plan. Example:

A security software start-up with no customers and an 'about-to-be-released' (Version 1.0) product was looking to get the first key clients in the door. Because the value propositions centered on meeting strict government security guidelines, the company concentrated on prospects in highly regulated industries, such as healthcare, utilities, finance, and government, where a breach in security meant the death of their business (the consumer products industry would have to wait). Further, because these first customers would likely endure some of the growing pains in partnership with the company (product hiccups, support challenges, etc.), the company wanted to work through some of these challenges with smaller customers and avoid 'stubbing-their-toe' with the biggest companies in each vertical market. However, in order to *eventually* seduce these bigger customers, the company would want credible and recognizable references within their vertical markets and would need to make sure the smaller customers they initially landed were solid brand names. Graphically, territory segmentation for this start-up security software company looking to land first customers would look like this:

Defined Market (Regulated Industries)

Vertical Markets (Healthcare, Utilities, Finance, etc.)

Sizing (Revenues, # Employees)

Brand Names (Strong Name Recognition)

Exhibit F—First Customer Segmentation Filter

Prospecting for Follow-On Customers: Having established a beachhead of initial customers, a company is likely to introduce more salespeople to the field. When looking for follow-on customers (new customers, but not the company's first customers), sales management should help the salesperson segment the territory by analyzing the customer base. Why are existing customers buying? Typically there are many forces at work:

- Product Leadership
- Need for Domain/Vertical Market Expertise (Consulting)
- Flexibility to Address Custom Requirements (Functionality, Service, etc.)
- Micro-Economics that Dictate the Need for the Solution (changes in legislation, natural disasters, fads, etc.)

Success with prospects is often as simple as this: *focusing on a value-proposition that resonates with, and can repeatedly be demonstrated to, a specific type of potential client.* Sales Management must encourage salespeople to be more 'pure' in the business they pursue, staying diligent in the pursuit of clients whose business model is similar to those that have demonstrated success with the solution. Sales Management also must make certain that salespeople are equally as diligent about **_not_** pursuing those clients with business models where they must 'bend' the value proposition and/or solution in order to make it work. Management should ensure that the salespeople have case studies from successful customers and replicate selling effort into similar accounts for quick-wins.

These follow-on customers would likely endure some of the growing pains in partnership with the company (product hiccups, support challenges, etc.), but not nearly to the degree of the initial customers. The salesperson can be more confident that some of the product and support 'bumps in the road' have been worked out with the early customers, and can begin to pursue some of the bigger companies in the vertical markets where the company has had success. The salesperson must to continue to focus on credible and recognizable brand-name references within those vertical markets to continue to leverage the customers they do land with future prospects. Graphically, territory segmentation for the salesperson pursuing follow-on customers would look like this:

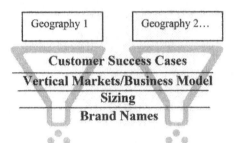

Exhibit G—Follow-On Customer Segmentation Filter

One interesting twist to pursuing follow-on customers is when there are existing relationships and a reputation in the territory from a prior salesperson. Example:

Early in my career, an associate and I inherited an abandoned sales territory. We studied the installed account base and planned to make an initial *tour-of-duty* to those accounts as soon as we entered the territory. Our initial goal of the tour of duty was to convince the customer that we intended to sell them *nothing*, and instead learn everything we could about the value they were deriving from our solution (and hence gauge their willingness to serve as a reference to other potential customers in the territory). This sounds contrary to the 'new territory, take no prisoners' approach of most sales teams, but it gave us a fast start to what ultimately resulted in our being the number one selling team in the company.

Prospecting for Follow-On Product Opportunities with Existing Customers: The salesperson prospecting for new opportunities in an existing customer base must revisit existing clients with some kind of "integration" or continuation strategy. Customers trust the company, no longer consider the salesperson's contact to be a "cold call", and are more likely to tell the salesperson what they think of the solution and spending more money with the company in a new way. Sales Management must help the salesperson segment their territory by dissecting the customer base using the following qualifiers:

- *Willingness to expand their relationship* with the company. These customers have likely endured some pleasure or pain in partnership with the company (product hiccups, support challenges, etc.), so the salesperson will need to measure the level of pain before suggesting an expanded relationship.

- *Ability to expand their relationship* with the company. Having the will/desire to expand their relationship with the company (above) is different than having the ability to do so. The salesperson will need to verify the customer's financial situation, payment history, etc. to warrant the effort to expand the relationship. Can the customer afford a broader relationship with the company?

- *Need for an expanded relationship* with the company. Do the additional solutions offered by the company augment what they already own from the company, or are the products unrelated and require a 'start from scratch' approach?

- *Credibility as a reference.* The salesperson must consider whether the effort to be put forward with certain customers in the territory will result in credible and recognizable brand-names to extol the virtue of (i.e., serve as a reference for) an expanded relationship with the company.

- *Likelihood that they will buy* from the company versus the competitor. When approaching customers with new solutions, salespeople have to be aware of *"Customer Predispositions":* the customer has favored (and bought from) the company's competitor in the past; friends/associates have attempted to sell them in the past and have relationships and/or information as to the customer's history of buying; a competitor has strong executive ties with the customer, etc.

Graphically, territory segmentation for the salesperson pursuing follow-on product opportunities with existing customers would look like this:

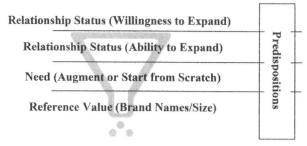

Exhibit H—Existing Customer Segmentation Filter

Most importantly, the ***tour-of-duty*** concept works famously when looking for new opportunities in the existing customer base. Sales Management must encourage the salesperson to go to the sponsor in the account (the person that has direct responsibility for either having bought the solution or for supporting the solution) and offer to FIX something. Even if the customer hasn't lodged a complaint since the day they bought the product, there's always something that can be fixed … relationships between the two companies, a past invoice, too many marketing e-mails, etc.). When the salesperson spends enough time fixing whatever problem the customer has (and they should fix it even if it isn't sales related), it will show a high-level of commitment to the customer's success, rather than just the salesperson's interest in earning the commissions from yet another product sale.

The result of the tour-of-duty is surprising:

- First, salespeople build relationships quickly that are built on trust. [By the way, relationships are the most under-rated aspect of selling. A friend and sales manager of mine used to take relationship-building so seriously that when we he went on first-time sales calls with his team, if the salesperson didn't spend the first several minutes trying to discover where the prospect grew up, went to school, had previous employment, etc. he had to buy the entire team dinner].

- Second, when the salesperson fixes something first, the conversations eventually shift to the *other* problems the organization is having that may relate to *other* products/solutions the salesperson has to offer. It's much like my motto on taking customers to events such as ballgames, etc.: 'He who speaks about business first loses'. I've always been amazed that when you are sitting next to a customer at a ballgame with your kids, and you just try to enjoy the game and make certain the customer is doing the same, how quickly the customer will get 'edgy' and inevitably bring up business. The same goes for doing the customer another favor of fixing a problem. When the customer is relaxed with the salesperson, the customer 'opens-up' about the need for the salesperson's products, value, internal adoption, success and visibility within the organization. This "indirect" method of selling— an innocuous tour-of-duty to ingratiate the salesperson to the customer by solving a problem they have with the company—is another way for the salesperson to gain access to information about other problems they can address in the future. Note: I said the future … *after* the salesperson has solved a problem.

Finally, when sales management is segmenting territories for **all three** scenarios above, they must certify that the prospect's business model suggests they will buy an external solution to solve their pain: *how do they make and treat money?*

- Are they a margin or a volume-based business (i.e., high-technology versus manufacturing or distribution)?
- What percent-of-spend is allocated to buying external solutions (i.e., 1% of revenues are typically allocated to spend on information technology in the grocery business versus 12% of revenues allocated to marketing solutions in the consumer product industry)?

Sales Managers must make certain that salespeople avoid spending time chasing companies that may need their product, but have a history of not allocating budget for it. In certain customer environments, if the product doesn't improve efficiency, save money, or directly have an impact on making money, the salesperson may as well move on. The salesperson will spend a great deal of time justifying a solution to people who won't get the CFO's approval to spend money on it. Make sure that as a sales manager, you've perused the salesperson's territory list and asked yourself if your company's product can help this company make or save money.

Chapter 6

Territory Planning: Build a Territory Plan

Audit Point:	A territory plan must exist for each sales territory. It should be a simple document with current and prospective accounts, focused on market, revenue estimates, prospecting and development plans.
Control Document:	Final Territory Plan.

In the last chapter, sales management verified through the Sales Audit that territories were segmented according to the company's current maturity and situation, and that salespeople were pursuing a list of companies that had a need for their solution. *The Sales Audit now examines whether the sales manager and salesperson have a general territory plan for approaching the accounts in the segmented territory.*

The plan must incorporate the segmentation criteria, account detail, and metrics which define success for prospecting and sales development in these accounts. It needs to be simple and identify three things:

1) **Here is how sales management and the salesperson will measure success**
2) **Here are the accounts that will determine the salesperson's (and the company's) success**
3) **Here are the salesperson's specific targets**

Nothing more sophisticated than that.

Managers have many salespeople to deal with effectively. Some may try to jam a specific 'territory plan format' down the throats of their salespeople, and with good intentions: when the manager has a small amount of time to try to determine whether the sales team is making progress, a simple form that baselines success the same way for every salesperson is a quick method for making that determination. But salespeople tend to fight the 'territory plan format' as mandated by sales management. To avoid this, sales managers should spend time validating that the form includes information that is also valuable to the salesperson in the field.

Territory plan formats are a dime-a-dozen. Sales Managers should choose one, and make sure that the one chosen is *one page*. Any territory plan that spreads over multitudes of pages becomes nothing more than an exercise in creative writing that ends up on the shelf or discarded. Sales Management should discuss the information with the sales team, and explain the reason they are trying to capture it (a quick conversation about it will yield the sales manager good ideas from a smart team). If the plan is simple to read and understand, it will become part of the salesperson's toolkit, become part of a defined process, and get integrated into the salesperson's performance review and improvement planning.

Exhibit I is a simple example of an initial territory plan:

Segmented Territory (Geography): Mountain Time Zone, (26) Fortune 1000 Accounts

Customer Base:	Case Study?	Troubled?	Lifetime Spend	Products
Adolph Coors (CO)	N	Y	$500,000	MP
Level 3 (CO)	Y	N	$3,000,000	Express
Questar (UT)	Y	Y	$250,000	Express
Motorola (AZ)	N	N	$2,750,000	XMT
Boise-Cascade (ID)	Y	N	$800,000	MP

Vertical Market/Business Model:	SIC Major	Minor
Food Processing	20	208
Communications	48	4813
Utilities	49	493
Electronics	36	-
Paper Products	26	267

Target List (26 Accounts):	Vertical Fit	Brand Name	Sizing	Predisposition
Salt River Project (AZ)	Y	N	Y	N
U.S. Airways (AZ)	N	Y	Y	Y
Corporate Express (CO)	N	Y	Y	Y
Utah Power & Light (UT)	Y	N	Y	N
J.R. Simplot (ID)	Y	Y	Y	Y
Questar (UT)	Y	N	Y	Y
Adolph Coors (CO)	Y	Y	Y	Y

Success Metrics:

Quota: $1,800,000

26 Target Accounts x 50% Customer Viability Estimate = 13 Opportunities in FY
13 Opportunities / 4 Quarters = 3 New Opportunities in Q1, Q2 & Q3; 4 in Q4

Average Selling Price = $200,000; Large Deal = $500,000; Small Deal = $100,000
Bell Curve on 13 Opportunities = 2 Small, 9 Average, 2 Large

(2 x $100,000) + (9 x $200,000) + (2 x $500,000) = $3,000,000 FY Pipeline
$3,000,000 Pipeline x 30% Close Rate = $900,000 (50% of Quota) in FY

Exhibit I—Initial Territory Plan

In the sample above, the salesperson will feel pain as the plan above yields less than the quota assignment. Sales Management must be open to the possibility that this will be the result of an initial territory plan, and in this example should discuss the assumptions and expectations with the sales person to decide on a more aggressive strategy (or, less likely, justify a quota reduction).

Once agreement is reached, expectations are set-out in the territory plan, and the execution of the plan (the activities behind building revenue and the pipeline) will need to be developed. Some examples of execution steps:

First, help the salesperson plan a 'tour of duty' for customer accounts (remember: fix a problem before trying to sell something). If *troubled* accounts are part of the revenue plan, they need to go first (i.e., Questar and Adolph Coors from the above example). Help the salesperson to be specific on plans to visit them and to set timetables. Name the account, the month in which the first visit will be made, and the target date for clearing up the situation. Next, do the same for *'non-troubled'* customers that provide an opportunity to generate more immediate revenue (i.e., Level (3), Motorola and Boise-Cascade from the above example). Agree on metrics on both. For example:

"[Salesperson] plans to visit the two troubled accounts in the first 90 days, with no expected revenue. [Salesperson] plans to visit the other 3 customers in the first 90 days to determine the depth of their use of the product. It's reasonable to believe [Salesperson] will generate one new opportunity from these 5 accounts".

Then have the salesperson document it on the territory plan:

Q1: Visit Troubled Accounts: Questar (January) and Adolph Coors (February)
Visit Existing (Non-Troubled) Customers: Level (3), Motorola and Boise-Cascade
Q2: Determine potential for New Opportunities in Troubled Accounts
(1) New Opportunity from Existing Customer Visits in Q1

Second, activity and metrics for 'Prospective' Accounts (accounts that are not already existing customers) should be similar to those of the customers in the salesperson's territory plan. Encourage the salesperson to start with those accounts that have a 'predisposition' to buy from your company (i.e., U.S. Airways, Corporate Express, and J.R. Simplot from the above example). Whatever the predisposition (they know the salesperson from a previous life, they hired an employee that bought your company's product at a previous employer, they sit on your company's board, etc.), help the salesperson leverage it to make prospecting easier. The expectations of activity and the expected yield are based on the salesperson's personal experience, and sales management should validate the expectations with input from the rest of the selling team in the field. They know the reality of coverage activities and supporting tools to accomplish it (marketing collateral, lead generation assistance, etc.). What management should expect to see from the salesperson submitting the territory plan is "aggressive reality". Some examples of territory plan action items for prospective accounts:

- Executive Letters
- Cold Calling (which requires a pre-defined script according to the company's value propositions)
- Case Studies (where other customers of similar type have been successful using the product that can be e-mailed to prospects)
- Upcoming Events
- Networking/References into Cold Calls/Visits
- Gimmicks (such as investing in executive promotional items that will help secure an appointment, such as sending a putter cover and offering the putter upon granting an appointment)
- Handwritten or a 'Post-It' Notes attached to pertinent industry articles, or
- Anything creative that differentiates the salesperson's offer from every other offer the prospective client receives.

Whatever the method, management wants to have an understanding of the salesperson's plan to get in the door, and that the salesperson considers it their personal responsibility to do so.

As part of the plan for coverage, sales management needs to be clear on the appropriate place to start within prospective organizations: which title/role should receive the message, and what method will the salesperson use to deliver it. This should be carried out according to timeframes and expected metrics: typical hit rate on cold calls and letters is very low, in the single-digit percentages (such as 2%). Corporate marketing efforts and events can achieve more in the low two-digit range (such as 12%). The results will depend on the effort the salesperson puts into researching recipients before the effort is made.

Because sales management has worked with the salesperson to identify key target accounts, it is best to make sure that salespeople are handed the 'baton of responsibility' for researching these accounts prior to prospecting. The more specific the knowledge of the account, the market, the account's mission statement, who the account competes with, and the issues the account faces, the better the salesperson will be able to articulate a value proposition and increase their 'hit rate'. For a public company, I always check the Letter to the Shareholders as a way to zero-in on the important issues that the prospects will be aligned with (see Chapter 7). For a private company it's a bit more difficult, but the same can be picked up by simple research of the industry and the company's website information on their mission in the industry. Trade journals will often highlight industry challenges, and often customer executives will appear in industry articles. Always make sure the salesperson uses an internet search engine to research the prospect's company and executives and to uncover an issue or 'connection' on which the salesperson can build a prospecting message. As a sales manager, look for detail that the salesperson can provide about specific accounts on their key target list and how the salesperson plans to penetrate the account using that information. A good salesperson will know (but all salespeople should be reminded), that detail around a territory plan will raise management's level of confidence in the salesperson's prospecting results.

As a sales manager, you should take responsibility for scheduling a 180-day check-up on the plan (pick a specific date), and helping the salesperson make any modifications to the general territory plan based on the results of that check-up. Take a stake in the success of the salesperson's execution.

Exhibit J is a finished example of a single-page territory plan:

Assigned Territory (Geography): Mountain Time Zone, 26 Fortune 1000 Accounts

Customer Base:	Case Study?	Troubled?	LTD Spend	Products
Adolph Coors (CO)	N	Y	$500,000	MP
Level 3 (CO)	Y	N	$3,000,000	Express
Questar (UT)	Y	Y	$250,000	Express
Motorola (AZ)	N	N	$2,750,000	XMT
Boise-Cascade (ID)	Y	N	$800,000	MP

Vertical Market/Business Model:	SIC Major	Minor
Food Processing	20	208
Communications	48	4813
Utilities	49	493
Electronics	36	-
Paper Products	26	267

Target List (26 Accounts):	Vertical Fit	Brand Name	Sizing	Predisposition
Salt River Project (AZ)	Y	N	Y	N
U.S. Airways (AZ)	N	Y	Y	Y
Corporate Express (CO)	N	Y	Y	Y
Utah Power & Light (UT)	Y	N	Y	N
J.R. Simplot (ID)	Y	Y	Y	Y
Questar (UT)	Y	N	Y	Y
Adolph Coors (CO)	Y	Y	Y	Y

Revenue Estimates:
Quota: $1,800,000
26 Target Accounts x 50% Customer Viability Estimate = 13 Opportunities in FY
13 Opportunities / 4 Quarters = 3 New Opportunities in Q1, Q2 & Q3; 4 in Q4
Average Selling Price = $200,000; Large Deal = $500,000; Small Deal = $100,000
Bell Curve on 13 Opportunities = 2 Small, 9 Average, 2 Large
(2 x $100,000) + (9 x $200,000) + (2 x $500,000) = $3,000,000 FY Pipeline

Prospecting Plan/Expected Results:

Visits/Week: 5 – 10

Q1: Visit Troubled Accounts: Questar (January) and Adolph Coors (February)
 Visit Existing (Non-Troubled) Customers: Level 3, Motorola and Boise-Cascade
 Executive Letter Campaign to prospects with predispositions (Corporate Express,
 U.S. Airways and J.R. Simplot) using Vertical Market-proven Case Studies
 Cold Calling Campaign into the 18 remaining accounts.
Q2: Determine Potential for New Opportunities in Troubled Accounts
 (1) new account opportunity from Customer Visits in Q1
 (1) new account opportunity from Executive Letter Campaign (30% hit-rate)
 (1) new account opportunity from Cold Calling Campaign (6% hit-rate)
Q3: Progress Check (July) with Sales Management

Exhibit J—Final Territory Plan

Chapter 7

Prospecting the Territory

Audit Point: Execute on the territory plan and measure the results. Adequately research the targets and find a creative way to gain access to the 'right' contacts with the 'right' message at the 'right' time.

Control Document: Call Sheet and Weekly Activity Sheet

The Sales Audit so far has identified and interrogated your company's processes for surveying to set sales expectations, using survey results to interview, hire and train salespeople in alignment with those expectations, segmenting territories to ensure efficiency in the salesperson's pursuit of potential customers, and building a general execution plan for that pursuit. *Now the Sales Audit requires that sales management examine the salesperson's execution on prospecting.*

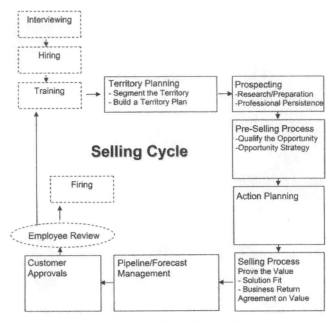

Exhibit E—The Selling Cycle

Frankly, sales managers know that prospecting is the part of the job that most salespeople avoid like the plague. Researching the target list of accounts, identifying the right contact within those accounts, and actually picking up the phone (or devising a campaign) to hunt the contact down has a certain 'stigma' for salespeople. It can be downright intimidating, especially for the salespeople who tend not to prepare very well for it.

Prospecting is something that companies and sales managers don't traditionally teach. If cold-calling means writing seductive e-mails and devising creative campaigns in order to succeed, and the company doesn't have training around cold-calling, then sales managers must make sure the hiring process yields people who have a history of success with these things (refer back to Chapter Two and add questions in the interview that will test for these skills).

There are all kinds of books on prospecting and cold-calling—how to sell in one call, how to talk to top officers, how to structure a conversation to get the interest of the person on the other end, how to make a conversation more casual, etc. The challenge in prospecting comes down to two things:

1) **The salesperson doing preliminary research on the account they are calling:**
   - **What the company does**

- How well they do it and why
- The challenges they (and or others in their industry) face doing it
- Companies like this that have had challenges and worked with our company to solve them

2) **Professional persistence (a true belief that what you offer provides benefit so that you achieve the 'Trifecta'):**
   - The Right Message
   - To the Right Person
   - At the right time

The biggest mistake a salesperson can make is to launch into prospecting with the following assumption: the receiver on the other end cares. The receiver has a **real job** and their own problems doing it. They get a myriad of phone messages, letters and e-mails every day and likely deep-six them all.

I once asked an executive who had agreed to meet with me why she took the call. Her answer was simple: *"because I am currently in the market for what you are offering".* Although I was under the delusion that my creativity and style had won the meeting, the truth sank in that I got the meeting because I had hit the **Trifecta** (right message, right person, and right time).

Is this purely luck? Most salespeople have had their manager say to them at one time or another that a good salesperson 'makes their own luck'. That's just another way of saying that the harder the salesperson searches for an appropriate selling opportunity, and prepares for making the initial contact, the more likely the salesperson is to find an opportunity. The work starts with the salesperson methodically researching the accounts in the territory plan. The sooner in the fiscal year that sales managers ensure that salespeople are doing this, the better the chances are that the sales team will deliver the right message to the right person at the right time.

Don't misinterpret the word 'research'. Finding out what a company does, how well they do it and why, and the challenges they face in doing it can be found in a couple of mouse-clicks or in a single trip to a prospect's lobby. One of the companies on the sample territory plan is Level (3) (a publicly held company). In the company's lobby were copies of their annual report. Reviewing a copy and the 'Letter to the Shareholders', a salesperson can be very well prepared for a meeting with the prospective customer. The following shows excerpts from the 'Letter to the Shareholders' in the annual report (Level (3) Communications Annual Report, 2003):

TO OUR STOCKHOLDERS:

[Last year] was an important year for Level (3), a year in which the company and its operating subsidiaries achieved a number of critical objectives and milestones.

Over the course of the year, ... we grew consolidated revenue by 29 percent ... while reaching positive consolidated free cash flow.... we reduced our outstanding debt by $850 million.

This year, we are continuing to take aggressive steps to ensure our success.... Among these is a major initiative to accelerate the rollout of new products and services.... In addition, we are investing in other important growth markets for communications....

We have the liquidity and resources available to invest in new market opportunities....

Our top customers include premier communications companies like America Online, AT&T, AT&T Wireless, Cable & Wireless, EarthLink, France Telecom, Microsoft, SBC, United Online and Verizon. During the year, we signed additional service agreements with a substantial number of leading companies, including Sony, PanAmSat, Cox Communications, Hughes Network Systems, BT, Sprint and Deutsche Telekom.

Since the beginning of [the year], we have also generated more than $120 million in cash through the continued sale of non-core assets, including:

- $46 million in January from the sale of Level3's interest in the "91 Express Lanes" toll road in Orange County, CA

GROWTH INITIATIVES AND NEW OPPORTUNITIES

... We have introduced a series of new services designed for both businesses and consumers ... Voice over IP (VoIP) services are a central focus ...

... We have significantly expanded our channel partner program.

INFORMATION SERVICES

A substantial majority of information services revenue came from Software Spectrum, our Dallas-based software distribution subsidiary. The remainder is attributable to (i)Structure, a provider of IT outsourcing solutions with operations in Colorado.

… As the cost of communications continues to fall, companies will increasingly be able to access these services remotely over broadband networks. We believe the combination of Level (3)'s continuously upgradeable network, and … expertise in software distribution and management, as well as strong customer relationships, position us to become one of the primary underlying backbone networks over which this kind of service is delivered …

The Letter to the Shareholders can be the **majority** of the research you will initially need to do. The next pages show how a sales manager can help a salesperson interpret the Letter to the Shareholder for use in prospecting:

TO OUR STOCKHOLDERS:

[This year] was an important year for Level (3), a year in which the company and its operating subsidiaries achieved a number of critical objectives and milestones.

[Sounds like they've been struggling a bit and have been watching specific metrics this year]

Over the course of the year … we grew consolidated revenue by 29 percent … while reaching positive consolidated free cash flow.… we reduced our outstanding debt by $850 million.

[The company is successful at selling product, but is not profitable and there's not a lot of cash-on-hand to be spent extravagantly. Any cash is going towards cleaning up debt … Take a quick look at the financials to make sure they will pass a credit check before the selling effort goes too far.]

This year, we are continuing to take aggressive steps to ensure our success.… Among these is a major initiative to accelerate the rollout of new products and services.… In addition, we are investing in other important growth markets for communications.… .

[The rest of the cash is likely being funneled into R&D and growth markets. Discuss our solutions as they pertain to managing product development and controlling product rollouts …]

We have the liquidity and resources available to invest in new market opportunities.…

[How can our solutions tie to the initiative of entering new markets?]

Our top customers include premier communications companies like America Online, AT&T, AT&T Wireless, Cable & Wireless, EarthLink, France Telecom, Microsoft, SBC, United Online and Verizon. During the year, we signed additional service agreements with a substantial number of leading companies, including Sony, PanAmSat, Cox Communications, Hughes Network Systems, BT, Sprint and Deutsche Telekom.

[Are any of these customers also OUR customers? Could they reach out to verify the success they are having with our solutions? Could we form a joint partnership to approach these clients together?]

Since the beginning of the year, we have also generated more than $120 million in cash through the continued sale of non-core assets, including:

- $46 million in January from the sale of Level3's interest in the "91 Express Lanes" toll road in Orange County, CA

[Further indication of their need to reduce debt and generate cash for pursuing new markets. What other businesses will they divest themselves of? Can our solutions help objectively evaluate and prioritize projects for divestiture? Find out how they do it today ...]

GROWTH INITIATIVES AND NEW OPPORTUNITIES

... We have introduced a series of new services designed for both businesses and consumers ... Voice over IP (VoIP) services are a central focus ...

[What are the challenges with bringing these new services to market, especially to consumers which it sounds like they're new at serving. Does our company need VoIP services? Perhaps we can hook them up with our internal communications buyers?]

... We have significantly expanded our channel partner program.

[How do they plan to handle this expansion? What are the potential challenges with serving more partners? Is there a service they provide to their partners that we can help manage or help provide?]

INFORMATION SERVICES

A substantial majority of information services revenue came from [our] Dallas-based software distribution subsidiary. The remainder is attributable to [our subsidiary providing] IT outsourcing solutions with operations in Colorado.

[Their software distribution subsidiary also carries our software line. If they buy our product, is there a way for them to buy it through their own subsidiary and save

money? Their IT outsourcing subsidiary is already a customer of ours … how closely do they work together? Could we expand that relationship to include Level (3)?]

… As the cost of communications continues to fall, companies will increasingly be able to access these services remotely over broadband networks. We believe the combination of Level (3)'s continuously upgradeable network, and … expertise in software distribution and management, as well as strong customer relationships, position us to become one of the primary underlying backbone networks over which this kind of service is delivered …

[How do we work with them on their broadband initiative? Can we help them be more efficient or provide a unique offering to broadband providers, or even customers?]

As you can see, the notes can now be consolidated to change the way your salesperson approaches this prospect/customer. Remember something:

Many annual reports are nothing more than marketing documents, and much of the information may either be quite out-of-date or put there simply to attract potential investors.

You'll have to work with the salesperson to give the information from the report the sniff-test (is this bologna or something the company really cares about) and validate it with other sources found on the internet. After all of your salesperson's efforts to validate the information, it may still end up being wrong. But, the salesperson will have shown effort and interest in the prospect's business, and it will be appreciated and recognized.

Assuming the information gathered passes muster, then the first question sales management needs to ask of the salesperson is this: given the notes above, who should you be calling on to discuss how you can help? Then you and/or the salesperson should formulate a call sheet based on extrapolations from your notes in order to make that call. Just take the notes and turn them into questions that will be asked, and action items that must be completed before the call, to make the call more productive. For example:

LEVEL (3)—CALL SHEET

Key: Q = Question; T = Task

[This year] was an important year for Level (3), a year in which the company and its operating subsidiaries achieved a number of critical objectives and milestones.

[Sounds like they've been struggling a bit and have been watching specific metrics this year]

Q: What are the financial objectives and metrics for this year?

Over the course of the year … we grew consolidated revenue by 29 percent … while reaching positive consolidated free cash flow.… we reduced our outstanding debt by $850 million.

[The company is successful at selling product, but is not profitable and there's not a lot of cash-on-hand to be spent extravagantly. Any cash is going to clean up debt … Take a quick look at the financials to make sure they will pass a credit check before the selling effort goes too far.]

T: Check financials and run an internal credit review.

This year, we are continuing to take aggressive steps to ensure our success.… Among these is a major initiative to accelerate the rollout of new products and services.… In addition, we are investing in other important growth markets for communications.… .

[The rest of the cash is likely being funneled into R&D and growth markets. Discuss your solutions as they pertain to managing product development and controlling product rollouts …]

We have the liquidity and resources available to invest in new market opportunities.…

[How can your solutions tie to the initiative of entering new markets?]

T: Prepare a sell-sheet on our New Product Development (NPD) solution and our go-to-market (G2M) solution.

Q: Are you continuing emphasis on R&D and NPD? Who within your organization might be interested in discussion our solutions in this area?

Our top customers include premier communications companies like America Online, AT&T, AT&T Wireless, Cable & Wireless, EarthLink, France Telecom, Microsoft, SBC, United Online and Verizon. During the year, we signed additional service agreements with a substantial number of leading companies, including Sony, PanAmSat, Cox Communications, Hughes Network Systems, BT, Sprint and Deutsche Telekom.
[Are any of these customers also OUR customers? Could they reach out to verify the success they are having with our solutions? Could we form a joint partnership to approach these clients together?]

T: Check our reference database for these client names, and validate their ability to be referenced with the salesperson. Share the list with Level (3)

T: Check into how these customers are using our products, and brainstorm on how this may pertain to Level (3)'s business model. If so, be prepared to discuss the idea of a joint G2M offering with Level (3)

Q: We have joint customers. Who within your organization might be interested in discussing potential G2M strategies with us?

Since the beginning of the year, we have also generated more than $120 million in cash through the continued sale of non-core assets, including:
- $46 million in January from the sale of Level3's interest in the "91 Express Lanes" toll road in Orange County, CA

[Further indication of their need to reduce debt and generate cash to pursue new markets. What other businesses will they divest themselves of? Can our solutions help objectively evaluate and prioritize projects for divestiture? Find out how they do it today ...]

Q: What was the business idea behind this investment?

Q: Why are you divesting yourself of this investment and what other businesses are likely to be divested?

Q: Our solutions help customers objectively evaluate projects in-process and their risk/return against business objectives. How does your organization objectively evaluate projects and determine their candidacy for divestiture?

GROWTH INITIATIVES AND NEW OPPORTUNITIES

… We have introduced a series of new services designed for both businesses and consumers … Voice over IP (VoIP) services are a central focus …

[What are the challenges with bringing these new services to market, especially to consumers which it sounds like they're new at serving. Does our company need VoIP services that I can suggest I hook them up with our internal communications buyers?]

Q: What are the challenges your organization is having with bringing new services to market?

Q: Are there any changes/impacts to your business when service consumers versus businesses?

T: Contact our IT/Communications Department to see if we are investigating VoIP Solutions, and if so share it with Level (3).

… We have significantly expanded our channel partner program.

[How do they plan to handle this expansion? What are the potential challenges with serving more partners? Is there a service they provide to their partners that we can help manage or help provide?]

Q: What are the challenges you are having with expansion of your channel partners?

INFORMATION SERVICES

A substantial majority of information services revenue came from [our] Dallas-based software distribution subsidiary. The remainder is attributable to [our subsidiary providing] IT outsourcing solutions with operations in Colorado.

[Their software distribution subsidiary also carries our software line. If they buy our product, is there a way for them to buy it through their own subsidiary and save money? Their IT outsourcing subsidiary is already a customer of ours … how closely do they work together? Could we expand that relationship to include Level (3)?]

Q: Your software distribution subsidiary carries our product line. If our solution is found to address any issues you are facing, would there be any cost-benefit from you purchasing the software from your own subsidiary?

T: Check our reference database for Level (3)'s outsourcing subsidiary, and validate their satisfaction with the salesperson. If positive, then ask the following question of Level (3):

Q: Your outsourcing subsidiary is a client of ours. How closely do you work with them? Would you be interested in speaking with them regarding how they are using our solution?

… As the cost of communications continues to fall, companies will increasingly be able to access these services remotely over broadband networks. We believe the combination of Level (3)'s continuously upgradeable network, and … expertise in software distribution and management, as well as strong customer relationships, position us to become one of the primary underlying backbone networks over which this kind of service is delivered …

[How do we work with them on their broadband initiative? Can we help them be more efficient or provide an offering unique to broadband providers, or even customers?]

T: Contact internal Product Marketing to explore the application of our solution to the broadband market. If applicable, share with Level (3).

The whole concept here is simple: the majority of preliminary research can be accomplished through a simple review of the Letter to the Shareholders or from similar 'internet-available' information. For a privately held company, find a publicly held company in the same market, get the Letter to the Shareholders out of their annual report, and extrapolate. You'll need to help your salespeople be assumptive when asking questions, as the information may not be exactly the same for the privately held company. Their research should be centered on *revealing corporate initiatives to which all purchase decisions will likely be tied.*

When corporations plan, it's done top-down. Shareholders want return, CEO's develop programs with key initiatives to deliver this return (typically either by driving top-line revenues and/or driving down costs to improve profitability and increase share price), and direct-reports to the CEO develop their business plans to support these programs. The plans of the direct-reports to the CEO typically consist of projects that are carried out by their staff. The staff will often evaluate products and services that deliver on the projects. <u>That</u> is where vendors/solution providers come in.

If your salespeople can't tie your solution to a top-level program or key initiative, it is likely they are wasting their time with something that won't fly once it reaches the CFO (or whoever owns the budget) because it isn't important enough to tie to the CEO's programs or Company's key initiatives.

In a salesperson's research and resulting call sheet, the sales manager needs to ensure that the salesperson has answers to the questions initially posed:

1) **The salesperson doing preliminary research on the account and contact they are calling:**
   - **What the company does**
   - **How well they do it**
   - **The challenges they face in doing it**
   - **Other companies like theirs that have had similar challenges and have worked with our company to solve them**

Even with these answers, the sales manager must help the salesperson hit the Trifecta (right message, right person, and right time). In doing research and developing the Call Sheet, the salesperson has significantly improved their chances over a non-researched, unprepared cold-call:

- Improved quality of the message because it ties to CEO programs and Company key initiatives (right message)

- Identified areas to ask for permission to speak with an appropriate person regarding specific challenges (finding the right person)
- Assured that the information assembled is either still current or will lead to discussion on what is important this year or next (right time)

The Call Sheet above resulted from a visit to a customer (Level (3)) in hopes of expanding the relationship. More often than not, your salespeople are researching and developing a call sheet in hopes of gaining access to a previously untapped account. In that case, the salesperson needs to take the Call Sheet and focus on the additional challenge of gaining initial access into an account for prospecting:

2) **Professional persistence with the right message (a true belief that what you have to offer has application and can provide benefit to the customer).**

One of the most important skills in an effective salesperson is 'professional persistence': the ability to convey passion for the message, combined with a conversational style and tone, to gain access. Can the salesperson comfortably open a conversation, be humble but passionate and sincere in their approach, use personality to endear the prospect, deliver a meaningful message, and finally ask a question that gets the prospect talking … hopefully even laughing. Can they do it many times over in search of the person who truly owns the pain and responsibility associated with what they are selling? Professional persistence will be required in order for the salesperson to end-up with the right person. Getting to the important person may take many approaches, and may need to start with the trusted advisor of the person they are trying to reach (as with me … read on).

I spent two and a half years as CEO of a small infrastructure service provider. On average, I received forty calls per week from salespeople. They never reached me. All calls and e-mails were first routed to my assistant so that she could filter them for solicitors. Out of the forty calls per week, one-hundred-sixty calls per month, targeted for me, I probably heard **two**. Remember the ratios of success we talked about when prospecting a territory? Single-digit response rates. In this case, I returned about 1% of the calls. Why? The caller didn't hit the 'Trifecta'. I had people on my team that should have received the call (I was the wrong person), so my assistant likely forwarded them on to someone else's assistant for filtering. Some of the calls had no bearing on our business (wrong message) or the callers mispronounced my name or my company's name, so my assistant got rid of it immediately. Some callers offered a solution to a problem we had already addressed (wrong time), so my assistant never forwarded it on.

Worse yet, some of the callers actually got through to my assistant live, and treated her disrespectfully, like some evil gatekeeper. They were blacklisted. You see, my assistant essentially *ran* the day-to-day workings of the company. She knew everyone in the organization and their priorities because she had an unbelievable 'clearance level': she and I prepared presentations for the board, re-wrote company business plans, set up conference calls on strategic topics (everything from new products to mergers & acquisition), and set my calendar (both internal and external) for meetings on all kinds of topics. If you don't think that made her an expert on the business, our priorities, and what I personally cared about, you're crazy. I trusted that if someone called with something compelling or actually sounded intelligent about what our company did and the problems we faced, she would get them through to me. I can think of only three vendors that actually made it to my desk in two-and-a-half years (and we ended up doing business with two of them).

I am a big fan of doing enough research to be dangerous, but not so much that it consumes a salesperson's time. I'm also a fan of humility; of a salesperson who is aware that no matter how much research they do, they can never know enough about my business to tell me how to run it. I appreciate the salesperson showing that they've done some homework, perhaps even enough to lead to a logical conclusion that there is some evidence of my need for their solution. Better yet, that they have spoken with my assistant (and I can validate it when I check it out) and she thought it was a good idea for us to spend a few minutes on the topic. It helps if the caller mentions the names of the other people in my organization or industry that they have contacted prior to bringing their message to me. These attempts, while keeping a friendly, often humorous tone are what usually get the 'call-back'. Mostly, just showing initiative in a humble and humorous way, and an effort to try other vehicles before just launching a call into the top, is what usually got the return phone call. I just wanted some effort.

As a CEO, my sales team tested me on this once. I was on the warpath to instill the concepts above in my company's sales team. I had no marketing budget and needed to develop executive marketing vehicles that struck pay dirt (both to generate leads and to validate the effectiveness of messaging for our product). I wanted the sales team to do some research on their top targets, develop an executive letter, and follow the letter with a call to the executive's assistant. A couple of weeks later I received a hand-written executive letter in the mail and decided to show it to the sales team as an example of what salespeople were doing effectively. I took it to our sales meeting and shared that I was likely to have my assistant set an appointment with the sender (should he actually execute on the promise to contact me as stated in his letter). The room went nuts. It turns out my sales team had developed the letter, and wanted to see if it would prompt a response. It did, and they successfully went on to drive their own campaigns that would lead to a record quarter.

Today there is an exhaustion of executive letters in use in the field, and a bunch of look-alike methods for prospecting. Salespeople should constantly experiment with prospecting vehicles and settle in on whatever works most effectively for them. From handwritten post-its notes attached to important industry articles, to embossed invitations (with response cards), to exclusive executive breakfast forums, etc; prospecting is less about the actual technique a salesperson uses and more about the research, logical evidence that the value proposition 'fits', chain of contact prior to a call into an executive, and the ability to stay humble, sincere and passionate through it all. Beyond that, some of it is luck, timing (calling before and after hours ... salespeople shouldn't expect to reach anyone important during business hours) and how the salesperson handles the first few seconds after the person picks up the phone. These things will determine whether there is a step two.

Tracking the successful execution against a salesperson's prospecting plan is critical. A vehicle sales management can use to challenge their sales team is the Activity Sheet (**Exhibit K**):

Weekly Activity Report

Week Ending (Friday): 11/4/2005
Salesperson: Johnson

	Account	Contact	Title	LOB	Vehicle Used	Result	Week Ending
Customers	Adolph Coors	William Hanley	VP	Marketing	Executive Letter	No Response	21-Oct
		Stacy Lyndale	Director	Quality	Event Invitation	Attending	4-Nov
	Level 3	Susan Porter	Director	Engineering	Cold Call	Meeting 11-11	4-Nov
		Myrna Michaels	Manager	Research	Cold Call	No Response	28-Oct
	Questar	Phil Blankenstein	SVP	Finance	Executive Letter	CFO Visit Scheduled	4-Nov
	Motorola	Craig Little	Manager	Customer Support	Cold Call	Sending Literature	28-Oct
	Boise-Cascade	Janet Gilgore	VP	MIS	E-Mail Introduction	No Response	28-Oct
Targets	Salt River Project						
	U.S. Airways	Anna Smythe	Manager	HR	New Product Ad	No Response	21-Oct
	Corporate Express						
	Utah Power & Light						
	J.R. Simplot	Samantha Tilton	Programmer	IT	E-Mail Introduction	No Interest E-Mail	4-Nov
Other	Blue Cross of WA	Robert Camden	VP	Claims Processing	Incoming Call	Meeting 11-11	21-Oct
	Fujitsu of America	Ravi Ganesh	Director	Engineering	Web Download	Phone Call Scheduled	28-Oct
Partners	Capson & Company	Cameron Spatz	Principal	NA		Joint Client List Review	

Weekly Totals

			% Goal
Week Ending	21-Oct	3	60%
Week Ending	28-Oct	4	80%
Week Ending	4-Nov	4	80%

Exhibit K—Weekly Activity Sheet

Territory and sales management tools should be simple, no more than one page, and meant for the sole purpose of creating an audit trail for the sales team.

The Activity Sheet must document the names and titles of the people contacted in the accounts, when the contact was made, the vehicles used, and the results. It will grow organically during the course of managing a territory, and at the end of a time period it will serve as proof that the salesperson has done their job against the expected metrics shown in the territory plan. The Activity Sheet will demonstrate that the territory is (or isn't) yielding results, and will eventually serve as input to the sales manager's review of the salesperson's performance. There is always the chance that despite a salesperson's best efforts, the value proposition and solution aren't resonating with targeted accounts in the territory. It is better to know this, document and discuss it, and clear the account from the prospecting list than to keep working the account. An account disqualified can be as useful as one qualified. That's the topic of the next chapter.

Chapter 8

The Pre-Selling Process: Qualifying the Opportunity

Audit Point: A legitimate opportunity is defined by Critical Business Issues (CBIs) identified through qualification. Verify that the CBIs reach high into the organization, that the owner of the CBI has a compelling event for finding an immediate solution, and that your solution can provide unique business value to address it.

Control Document: Call Sheet and the 5P Sheet.

The Sales Audit so far has identified and interrogated your company's processes for surveying to set sales expectations, using survey results to interview, hire and train salespeople in alignment with those expectations, segmenting territories to ensure efficiency in the salesperson's pursuit of potential customers, building a general execution plan for that pursuit, and examining the salesperson's execution on prospecting. *The Sales Audit now shifts from interrogating the process of preparing for the sale into interrogation of the process of selling. Sales Management must examine how well the sales team qualifies opportunities in order to maximize selling productivity.*

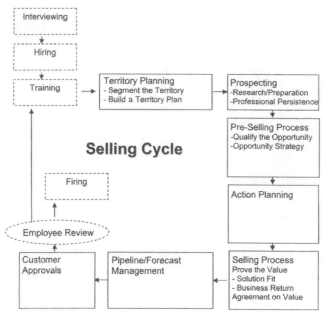

Exhibit E—The Selling Cycle

If sales management were to survey salespeople in the field about the most time-consuming and laborious steps in a sale, they might find that salespeople believe the closing step is the one that takes the most work, or the "value demonstration" step where countless demonstrations or presentations need to be done in order to overcome competition. The step that **should** take the most time, however, is the step that is most often dismissed: qualifying the opportunity.

The 'meat' of the Selling Cycle, and typically where sales management is deeply involved with the sales team and their opportunities, is in three logical sections:

- Pre-Selling Process (Qualify the Opportunity, Opportunity Strategy)
- Action Planning
- Selling Process (Prove the Value: Solution Fit, Business Return)

In this chapter, we're going to focus on Pre-Selling: *activity required to legitimize an opportunity.* Note the word 'legitimize'. Determining the legitimacy of an opportunity is the purpose of qualification.

Companies bear the cost of pursuing a selling opportunity, and yet the salesperson typically owns the responsibility for initiating pursuit. This is quite a degree of empowerment and shows a level of confidence in the salesperson by the company. The salesperson needs to ponder this because the company is counting on this empowerment and investment to pay off. The problem is that most salespeople don't see the qualifications module as part of the process they've been empowered to execute on the company's behalf. Qualification is where the salesperson will determine the amount of personal effort and company money they will spend on a chance at payback. If the salesperson spends time and the company's money on opportunities that are not legitimate, three things occur:

- The deal is not likely to close because the customer is indifferent to the solution.
- The salesperson is going to be frustrated and disappointed given the amount of effort they expend without reward.
- The company is going to question the confidence they have placed in the salesperson to perform as expected and will realize a lack of return on their investment.

Each selling opportunity should be considered its own simple risk/reward scenario: how much time will the salesperson spend pursuing a deal, and what is the likely outcome (not just to **win** a sale, but to win one of a size/magnitude that delivers a reasonable return on the company's/salesperson's investment)? The better an opportunity is qualified, the more legitimate the company's opportunity, and the more likely a positive return will result.

If an opportunity is appropriately qualified, there is a powerful and positive downstream impact:

Qualified → Customer Feeling Pain and Urgency → Salesperson helps Customer Define What is Required to Remove the Pain → Salesperson Quickly Demonstrates How the Solution Uniquely Meets the Requirements to Remove the Pain → Customer Understands Relief from Pain Available by Implementing the Solution → Customer Invests in Solution.

Without qualification, here's the negative downstream impact:

Not Qualified → Customer Feeling No/Dull Pain → Customer Lacks Urgency to allow Salesperson to help Define what is Causing the Pain → Salesperson Shows Solution Addressing no Specific Requirements, but trying to Intensify Dull Pain → Salesperson Shares Stories of Solution Solving Other Customer's Pain → Customer Understands the Pain of the Other Customer, but doesn't Empathize (now loops multiple times … ──┘

… until) → Salesperson Discounts Solution to 'Account For' a Dull Pain → Customer's Budget Holder asks Why the solution is Required at <u>Any</u> Price → Opportunity Dies (Elapsed Time: days, weeks, months).

A friend of mine, who held the title Chief Strategist at our mutual employer, lovingly coined this type of selling the 'L-T-D Method: Lead → Trial → Discount'. If there was a lead, it was simply taken at face-value to be a legitimate opportunity. Without digging into the requirements, the solution was put into the hands of the customer (i.e., a 'trial') hoping they would find reason to buy it. If the customer thought it was a nifty product, but it didn't solve a significant problem, the salesperson simply discounted it enough to convince the customer that it was an inexpensive gadget worth having. The 'trials' were never easy, the discounts always steep, and the answer always 'No' when it hit the desk of the budget-owner because there was no significant business case to justify the expenditure.

If the salesperson goes deep into the prospect's needs, the executive support their contact within the account has for acquiring a product, how they plan to evaluate products to meet their needs, or whether there is a budget at all for acquiring such a product, the answers are often vague and non-committal. The typical salesperson will not second-guess vague answers, but instead will keep digging through the haystack to find the needle (especially when the salesperson is dealing with contacts who are at lower levels within the account). Salespeople tend to jump to the conclusion that if someone says there is a need, then there must be a budget and project established in order for them to voice the need, making this opportunity 'qualified'. Sales Management can play a critical role in helping salespeople avoid the temptation to form such a conclusion.

The timing of qualifying an opportunity can also make salespeople very edgy. It absolutely must be done upfront, and sales management must ensure that the salesperson is verifying that the pain being addressed travels high into the organization. Salespeople are often concerned that verifying how high the pain occurs in the organization will make their lower-level contacts especially 'edgy', as these contacts don't want to expose their pain to their management too early or have to deal with their management's questions about their ability to 'deal with pain' without spending sparse company dollars. Without sales management's help in verifying how high the pain travels within the organization, the salesperson will forego making their low-level contact 'edgy', and likely fall into the trap of believing their contact's claims that they "have responsibility for making the decision" or are "working with all of the other competitors" on the same opportunity. The salesperson figures if the competitors are involved, or the low-level person is empowered to make a decision, all need to further qualify the opportunity is off the table. The salespeople themselves often get 'edgy' about qualification, because cutting through all of the issues above can mean that a deal will slow-down (or need to go backwards to revisit issues of qualification) before it can be legitimized. The salesperson sees this as the kiss-of-death when trying to convince management that they are capable of progressing opportunities and bringing short-term revenue home.

This couldn't be further from the truth. Every sales manager has countless examples of opportunities where a salesperson spent a plethora of resources to pursue a deal, only to come up empty as budgets vanished (or were found to never exist), executive sponsors changed (or never had) priorities, the competition undercut the price, etc. Salespeople should consider the process of qualification to be as much about **disqualifying** an opportunity as it is about **qualifying** an opportunity. Disqualification conserves the salesperson's time and the company's money:

- The salesperson avoids the practice of Ghost busting: chasing opportunities where there is a ghost-of-a-chance of actually selling something
- The company avoids the cost of supporting the salesperson in their chase
- The salesperson gets the peace-of-mind that this opportunity, in this account, is no longer part of the 'potential' that management believes exists in their territory (which will become critical at performance-review time)
- Frees the salesperson up to find legitimate opportunities they can win.

So why do salespeople spend so little time on qualifying an opportunity? Because the **downside** of completely qualifying an opportunity (if there is such a thing) is that the salesperson will have to make a bunch more cold calls in order to find something else to work on.

One of the quickest ways for a salesperson to run into trouble is for the salesperson (and the sales management) to give into the temptation that "working on something is better than working on nothing" or, more specifically "calling on someone you know, to work on something that might come up, is better than cold-calling a stranger to end up working on nothing". When the salesperson gives-in to this temptation, there is benefit in being out of the office, out of the line-of-fire of management. The salesperson successfully fills-up the day with a chain of e-mails sharing a wealth of information and countless versions of unsolicited proposals in an effort to turn the customers "interest" into pain. The customer figures that if the salesperson is willing to spend the time educating them (and they assume the salesperson knows there is no chronic pain), then they're willing to spend the time gaining expertise in this product area in order to further their ambition for the next great job or promotion. The salesperson is convinced that the customer (ole-buddy, ole-pal) wouldn't drag them along if there weren't a true need for the solution. Pushing back to truly qualify the need would insult the customer's (ole-buddy, ole-pal) integrity, potentially stop the flurry of activity, and force the salesperson back to the phones to prospect for something else (which is a lot less fun than speaking with people who genuinely seem to have an interest, and, frankly, will return their calls and go to lunch with them rather than give them the cold shoulder). It's understandable that the salespeople that give into the "working an unqualified opportunity is better than cold-calling" temptation look up at the end of every quarter and wonder why their pipeline is not yielding sales or why the opportunities in their pipeline always seem to stagnate at about the same stage in the selling cycle (see the 'loop' above).

The first step for sales management to help a salesperson that in this 'qualification denial' is to get them to admit they have a problem. The second step is for sales management to commit themselves and their team to the following philosophy: working on fewer, qualified opportunities is better than chasing a large number of unqualified opportunities.

Good qualification comes down to this: Identify a *Critical Business Issue (CBI)* in the organization, and travel up the corporate ladder to find the *highest ranking executive* who has *responsibility* for it, the *urgency* to solve it, and the *ability to make the decision*. The CBI must have corporate relevance (i.e., relate to a corporate initiative) and must be near the top of the highest ranking executive's agenda in order to be a legitimate opportunity worth chasing. I said nothing of defining requirements and nothing of drumming up interest across the organization. None of that matters until the salesperson gets to the person who is in so much pain because of the problem, that they are convinced something must occur to make the pain go away.

A Critical Business Issue is a problem that asks: ***what happens to the individual or the organization if this problem is not solved?***. It needs to be quantifiable and related to success metrics (such as % increase in revenue, % decrease in cost, or a reduction in risk or in cycle-time) or specifically qualifiable (such as an obvious increase in competitive advantage, required compliance with regulatory policy, or an improvement in analyst public opinion). To find CBIs, you begin with the line of questioning we've assembled in the previous chapter on the Call Sheet. We simply strip-out the questions resulting from our research to identify potential CBIs:

LEVEL (3)—CALL SHEET

Q1: What are the financial objectives and metrics for this year?

Q2: Are you continuing emphasis on R&D and NPD? Who within your organization might be interested in discussion our solutions in this area?

Q3: We have joint customers. Who within your organization might be interested in discussing potential G2M strategies with us?

Q4: I live in Orange County and actually drive this corridor. What was the business idea behind this investment?

Q5: Why are you divesting yourself of this investment and what other businesses are likely to be divested?

Q6: Our solutions help customers objectively evaluate projects in-process and their risk/return against business objectives. How does your organization objectively evaluate projects and determine their candidacy for divestiture?

Q7: What are the challenges your organization is having with bringing new services to market?

Q8: Are there any changes/impacts to your business when service consumers versus businesses?

Q9: What are the challenges you are having with expansion of your channel partners?

Q10: Your software distribution subsidiary carries our product line. If our solution is found to address any issues you are facing, would there be any cost-benefit from you purchasing the software from your own subsidiary?

Q11: Your outsourcing subsidiary is a client of ours. How closely do you work with them? Would you be interested in speaking with them regarding how they are using our solution?

Although a salesperson's initial access into an organization will likely not be with the highest ranking executive, the questions above are applicable to any-level contact. Why?

- They are questions generated from their Annual Report, and arguably any employee will have an interest in them or perhaps even have their own daily tasks tied to projects related to the corporate initiatives named in the report.
- If the contact is unable to answer/discuss these questions, it is a perfect opportunity to ask for their support in gaining access at a higher level without just blindly going around them (and potentially losing their support in the future).

Essentially everything that is a CBI (especially given that our goal is to validate the CBI with the highest ranking executive responsible for it) will boil down to quantification against the only metrics that an executive cares about:

$$P = (R - E): T: K$$

Where P = Profit, R = Revenue, E = Expense, T = Time and K = Risk. If pain or a need is not negatively impacting Profit, it isn't attracting enough attention at the executive level to warrant using resources to eliminate it. Even CBIs that have qualifiable rather than quantifiable benefit (such as compliance with regulatory policy) have risk and expense implications. If the CBI doesn't relate to a corporate initiative that impacts the formula above, then the pain/need is likely not a CBI, and a solution for it would be categorized as '**nice-to-have**'. Nice-to-Have solutions often receive only limited attention and discretionary resources. When completely qualifying an opportunity, salespeople should focus on tangible, quantifiable benefits that have an impact on business metrics.

What do CBIs look and sound like? Let's take our Call Sheet as an example, and make the assumption that we're able to use this Call Sheet with the highest ranking officer to explore CBIs. Here are some examples of responses we might receive from our Call Sheet questions:

LEVEL (3)—CALL SHEET

Q1: What are the financial objectives and metrics for this year?

A1: Continue consolidated revenue growth by 30 percent, continue positive consolidated free cash flow and achieve profitability, further reduce outstanding debt by an additional $500 million.

Q2: Are you continuing emphasis on R&D and NPD? Who within your organization might be interested in discussion our solutions in this area?

A2: New product development and introduction is pivotal to our competitive advantage. We anticipate rollout of a new product each quarter this year, resulting in multiple development projects and marketing campaigns. Head of Research is Myrna Michaels, Head of Development is Susan Porter.

Q3: We have joint customers. Who within your organization might be interested in discussing potential G2M strategies with us?

A3: I am not familiar enough with your products to know how we might work together, but Steven Slagmont is our Chief Marketing Officer.

Q4: I live in Orange County and actually drive this corridor. What was the business idea behind this investment?

A4: Communications often leverages existing infrastructure for rights of thoroughfare. We invest in highways, tunnels, pipelines, waterways and other infrastructure projects to allow for ease of gaining rights to piggyback our wires, cable and fiber.

Q5: Why are you divesting yourself of this investment and what other businesses are likely to be divested?

A5: Anything non-core to our rollout of new products is a candidate for divestiture. We will likely use partnerships to supplement areas where we might have invested in the past.

Q6: Our solutions help customers objectively evaluate projects in-process and their risk/return against business objectives. How does your organization objectively evaluate projects and determine their candidacy for divestiture?

A6: An Executive Project Review Committee keeps project cost/benefit information current, and brings this information to a weekly project status meeting. These can take many hours to complete, and decisions are rarely unanimous. We don't do this well, and we need to improve in order to find ways to free-up budget to drive new products.

Q7: What are the challenges your organization is having with bringing new services to market?

A7: Internal communication between product idea generation, development, testing, quality, marketing and sales is very disjointed and manual. We often promise new product launches to customers in order to stay in front of competitors, only to miss the launch date. This can cost us millions in marketing spend.

Q8: Are there any changes/impacts to your business when service consumers versus businesses?

A8: The entire marketing and selling process is different.

Q9: What are the challenges you are having with expansion of your channel partners?

A9: In order to keep the attention of partners, we have to train them effectively, communicate with them during the new product launches, and support them technically when they have customer issues. We currently have a very small team running these functions, and scale is an issue.

Q10: Your software distribution subsidiary carries our product line. If our solution is found to address any issues you are facing, would there be any cost-benefit from you purchasing the software from your own subsidiary?

A10: Absolutely. We have cost advantages when we supply product to ourselves.

Q11: Your outsourcing subsidiary is a client of ours. How closely do you work with them? Would you be interested in speaking with them regarding how they are using our solution?

A11: So we're already a client? Our outsourcing subsidiary is our most profitable business as many more customers are looking to outsource non-core business processes, such as manufacturing. If you're helping us serve this growing business, I should understand how as we're looking to grow this business exponentially.

If these were the answers the salesperson received when using the Call Sheet in a customer meeting, this would have been one great sales call! The salesperson focused on business issues, and hit on several key initiatives using simple information from their research. But where are the obvious CBIs? There are some real CBI gems hidden in here:

A1: Continue consolidated revenue growth by 30 percent, continue positive consolidated free cash flow and achieve profitability, further reduce outstanding debt by an additional $500 million.

Grow revenues; get profitable; reduce debt. If the stuff the salesperson is selling doesn't map back to these initiatives somehow, there is no case for purchase. The salesperson will need to speak to some folks further down the ladder to determine which projects, in particular, are branching off of these key initiatives to deliver results.

A2: New product development and introduction is pivotal to our competitive advantage. We anticipate rollout of a new product each quarter this year, resulting in multiple development projects and marketing campaigns. Head of Research is Myrna Michaels, Head of Development is Susan Porter.

Well, the salesperson can start with Myrna and Susan. They will clearly have a bunch of projects around new product development and rollout that will drive marketing campaigns which should, in turn, drive revenue growth. Now the sales effort has identified some specific people that can help in a way that will map back to the key initiatives (the Trifecta: right message, right people, and right time). Susan will likely have a CBI of her own: drive quarterly product rollouts more profitably.

A6: An Executive Project Review Committee keeps project cost/benefit information current, and brings this information to a weekly project status meeting. These can take many hours to complete, and decisions are rarely unanimous. We don't do this well, and we need to improve in order to find ways to free-up budget to drive new products.

The executive has a CBI from the answer above: free-up budget for new products by improving the process through which we evaluate projects for divestiture. Once the salesperson defines who is on the Project Review Committee, the issue of 'objective evaluation of projects' should be discussed and how the salesperson's solution can help facilitate it.

A7: Internal communication between product idea generation, development, testing, quality, marketing and sales is very disjointed and manual. We often promise new product launches to customers in order to stay in front of competitors, only to miss the launch date. This can cost us millions in marketing spend.

The executive's CBI from this answer: improve internal communication to hit product launch dates and save millions in marketing spend. The salesperson should explore the potential to help with this issue and have the executive make introductions to the rest of the folks involved. Now, as an exercise, go back and translate A9 and A11 into CBIs on your own.

There will be some CBIs that a salesperson will gather directly from the executive, and others that the executive intimates and will need to be validated by the highest ranking executive's direct reports. The salesperson may even need to go down another level to the direct reports OF the direct reports. The key is to define the projects that link to the key initiatives, and to determine whether there is a way to positively impact these projects and the results.

So far, the process of uncovering business pain and CBIs has been performed top-down (starting with the highest ranking executive and using the results of the conversation to go down the ladder to find projects that will relate to the initiatives set by that executive). This process can also be performed bottom-up, starting with those individuals tasked with projects, attempting to find the pain they are having in delivering on those projects, and then relating their pain back to the initiatives the salesperson defined through research. The salesperson can then meet the highest ranking executive after-the-fact to discuss the challenges identified at the project level. Here's an example of a simple set of questions that I used to qualify opportunities for a resource management solution sold bottom-up in one of my previous territories:

1) How do you consolidate, manage and measure demand for resources today?
2) How do you prioritize strategic projects and apply resources objectively?
3) How do you manage resources, costs, benefits and risks across multiple projects in real time? How do you manage resources that are used for strategic AND tactical work?

Of course, these qualifying questions promoted all kinds of further conversations, and led to discussions about how resources mapped to the key initiatives of the company (i.e., outsourcing non-core resources to reduce cost, applying more resources to revenue generating projects and scrapping non-revenue generating ones, etc.). The answers were a great start to my conversation with executives in an effort to qualify the opportunity.

Rick Page is the author of the book "Hope is Not a Strategy" (McGraw-Hill, 2002) and CEO of The Complex Sale, Inc. John Geraci, one of the principals at The Complex Sale, Inc. (www.complexsale.com) developed a technique for uncovering a CBI when qualifying an opportunity during a sales call. Simply stated, if the salesperson hasn't done the research necessary to prepare a Call Sheet on the account (for reasons such as it is a spontaneous incoming call, the call occurs on the floor of a trade show, or the famous elevator or plane ride that puts a salesperson in the seat next to an unsuspecting prospect), the salesperson simply looks at their hand, separates their five fingers, imagines the letter 'P' on each fingertip, and asks the corresponding 'P' question:

1) Pain   (What are some of the job-pains this person feels every day?)
2) Power   (Who has the authority to evaluate solutions to relieve the pain?)
3) Process   (What process is used to evaluate solutions?)
4) Preference (Is there a pre-disposition to any potential solution providers?)
5) Plan   (What is the plan for getting started?)

Exhibit P (I skipped a few letters, but thought the letter was appropriate) is a modification to The Complex Sale, Inc.'s RADAR sheet used by their own instructors, and can be used in a pinch to ferret-out answers using the 5P's technique above. The most important questions are obviously #2 and #3, as they meet the task of identifying the CBI head-on:

Name, Title & Position in the Organization Chart   **(Build Rapport: previous jobs, companies, hometown, schools, etc.)**
What is the person's <u>Pain</u>? (Why did this person agree to spend time with you?)
Is the pain a Critical Business Issue (what happens if the pain is not addressed)?
What is the person's responsibility and authority (<u>Power</u>) to solve the pain?
How high does the pain and responsibility for the pain go? (Who else in the "Pain Chain" has the power to say "No"?)
What is this person's <u>Process</u> for finding a solution to the pain?
What is the company's Process to evaluate and procure solutions for the pain?
Does this person or anyone in the pain chain have pre-disposition (<u>Preference</u>) to solution providers?
What <u>Plan</u> can we put in place to track our progress in the process?

Exhibit P—The 5 P's for Running a Sales Call (The Complex Sale, Inc.)

CBIs can be found at high and low levels within the organization. In order to truly be worthy of a salesperson's time and company's money, there must be quantifiable pain that links back to key company initiatives. There are three attributes of key company initiatives that make this linkage important:

- Executive Sponsorship (likely a change agent that has company credibility)
- Funding (solutions to deliver on key initiatives get funded)
- Urgency (key initiatives, unless they are multi-year programs, take priority)

So let's review how a sales manager can help a salesperson achieve complete and solid qualification:

Good qualification comes down to this: identify a *Critical Business Issue (CBI)* in the organization, and travel up the corporate ladder to find the *highest ranking executive* who has *responsibility* for it, the *urgency* to solve it, and the *ability to spend* their own money on it. A Critical Business Issue is a problem that is answered with the following question: ***what happens to the individual or organization if they don't solve this problem***.

By using our research to develop a Call Sheet, or in a pinch using the 5P sheet, the salesperson has a series of questions (for a top-level executives or lower level contacts) that will help to reveal CBIs (top-down), or key initiatives lower in the organization that can be linked back to CBIs (bottom-up). If the salesperson has done a good job of identifying the key initiatives and CBIs, they will understand the impact to the individual or organization of not eradicating the pain/CBI (and the quantifiable repercussions).

Will every opportunity a salesperson chases be fully qualified? No. But once the effort is made to fully qualify the opportunity, the sales manager and salesperson can jointly make an educated decision on whether to pursue it anyway. If the salesperson decides to get involved in a selling opportunity that is not fully qualified, it is critical to attempt to re-qualify at every step and get executive affirmation of the pain and the desire to spend budget to solve it.

This step in the Sales Audit asks sales management to examine how salespeople are qualifying opportunities to ensure that the time they spend pursuing them will net results. Chances are that there will be significant areas for improvement in the qualification step, as it tends to be one of the weakest skills of most sales teams. But eventually, sales managers build a team of salespeople that are skilled at recognizing the right opportunities on which to spend time, and the next step in a Sales Audit is to investigate whether the salespeople are formulating a plan of attack for moving these opportunities through to closure.

Chapter 9

The Pre-Selling Process: Opportunity Strategy

Audit Point: Once qualified, the opportunity must have an associated Strategy that is used for documenting what is known, and unknown, about the opportunity.

Control Document: Opportunity Strategy.

So a member of the sales team has a legitimate opportunity. The Sales Audit will reveal whether the sales manager has a process for building a strategy, enforces the execution of the strategy, and communicates on the effectiveness and potential changes required of the strategy to move the opportunity to closure. When you discuss the need for a strategy and regular review sessions with a salesperson, however, the salesperson's translation is typically negative: "my boss now wants to micro-manage me" or "the executive team wants to put their fingerprints on the deal so they can either claim credit or lay blame". However, experience demonstrates that the salesperson learns the most about how to close an opportunity, and how to manage future opportunities, when they proactively build a strategy and avoid having to reactively build one in response to a sale-in-trouble. It's an opportunity for the salesperson and sales manager to step away from the tree and take a look at the forest.

Exhibit E—The Selling Cycle

This next step of the Sales Audit requires sales management to help a salesperson become introspective and objective about an opportunity, and help them build a strategy that focuses not on what the salesperson knows about an opportunity, but rather what they don't know. There's a grid that identifies a salesperson's affinity for strategy and ability to objectively identify unknown aspects of the opportunity that will affect how they execute the sales process. I call it the 'Conscious-Competence Model', and every sales manager should privately evaluate each member of the sales team against it before building a strategy:

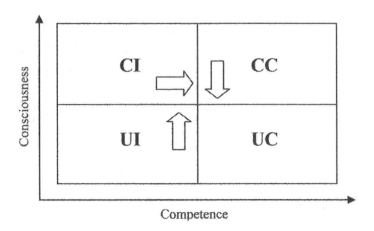

Legend: First Letter = Consciousness (C = Conscious, U = Unconscious)
       Second Letter = Competence (I = Incompetent, C = Competent)

Exhibit Q—Conscious Competence Learning Model (Howell and Fleischman, 1982)

The most dangerous salesperson is the Unconscious Incompetent (UI); a person that has absolutely no idea why they are unsuccessful at selling. This salesperson takes no time to reflect on their actions, determine if their actions are bringing them closer to achieving their goals, or whether they should modify their behavior to yield different results. UI's do not make good strategic salespeople, as they are not innately equipped to analyze the downstream impact of their actions.

Conscious Incompetents (CI) are initially no more effective in selling than UI's, but they know it. They have trouble making corrections to their strategy without someone walking them through the effects of experimentation and reasoning. The CI will be able to retrace their steps, and typically can tell you where they went wrong, but they'll need some help pulling together a way to improve or rethink the situation. Conscious Incompetents are very analytical, are very good planners and thinkers, but likely not good at execution. They will see the forest, but often will have trouble navigating through the trees. **Too much thinking** is as much a curse to the CI as **not thinking at all** is a curse to the UI. The positive aspect here is that CIs can be taught, as long as sales management has the time and patience.

The Conscious Competent (CC) is a salesperson that is conscious of every action they take, deliberates each step, and uses 'brute force' to complete each task. The Conscious Competent may approach similar situations differently, even if they have been more successful with one approach over another. CCs are "learning analytics", thinking through problems and weighing the consequences of their actions. They test theories and interpret results. The CC has been successful in the past, which tends to be less of a problem for a sales manager, but success does not come naturally or easily. The CC will require a lot of coaching, reassurance and often will require 'another set of eyes' on a problem.

The Unconscious Competent (UC) is a salesperson that is consistently successful because the process of selling comes naturally. The UC has internalized a successful process, and executes without too much contemplation. The UC subconsciously evaluates a situation, makes a plan, takes a course of action, understands why it does/doesn't work, automatically adjust to the results, takes another course of action, and repeats.

So why the importance of intellectual traits when it comes to strategy? Because for sales management to strategize with members of their teams, they must know with whom they are working. CCs can take the time to build a deep, multi-stage plan and keep it current as they execute. UI or CI's will likely need to be given tactical plans, shown how the tactics relate to the strategy, and discuss the outcomes before and after each action. UCs often won't do much documented planning at all, but will execute predictably and likely won't call on the sales manager much (which might drive a controlling manager nuts). Managers likely will have to spend more time with CI's and CC's observing the steps they take and explaining why the steps are/are not effective. The sales manager will need to offer alternative steps, work to document tasks in a formal action plan, and refer to the document regularly as a 'working example' to ensure that execution occurs now and is repeatable in the future.

Sales Management is effectively trying to move salespeople with various intellectual competencies through the 'Conscious-Competence Model' when working with them to build strategies. Strategizing will take many forms based on personality type, but the eventual goal is to help salespeople develop from their current-state into Unconscious Competence according to the path of the arrows in the **Exhibit Q** above.

Sales Managers can start by dealing with an issue common to all conscious-competence types: **having and executing on** a strategy. The sales manager should provide a tool to keep all salespeople's efforts linear and in sync with the desired outcome. **Exhibit R** is an example of that tool, called an Opportunity Strategy Template:

DynaCo – Data Center Consolidation Project

Deal Size	-	$150,000
Products	-	MXPress
Close Month	-	December

- **Critical Business Issue(s), Funding**
  - CIO has committed a FY 7% decrease in hardware capital spending and a 10% decrease in IT expense allocation to CFO
- **Org Charts, Top-Down/Bottom-Up Impact**
  - CIO reports to CFO
  - VP of IT reports to CIO
  - Data Center Manager reports to VP/IT
- **Compelling Event**
  - Budgeting Process completes this quarter
  - 60% of CIO and Staff MBOs rely on results
- **Competition, Predispositions**
  - In-House Consolidation
  - FGH, Incorporated
- **Activity Plan, Decision Criteria**
  - (Attached)

- **Unique Technical Value, Requirements List**
  - Multi-Platform Hardware Consolidation
- **Unique Business Value, ROI**
  - Hardware Re-financing Incentives
- **Issues/Obstacles**
  - Prior Product Challenges
  - Credit Qualification
- **Selling Team Members**
  - Sam Wilson, CFO
  - Regional Solution Partner
  - Professional Services
  - System Engineers
  - Product Management

Exhibit R—Opportunity Strategy Template

This Opportunity Strategy should be built by each salesperson for every legitimate opportunity, and sales managers should plan to help build the original strategy as well as revisit it dozens of times with the salesperson throughout its execution. Focusing on the example above and each element therein, here are the questions to ask when building the template with the salesperson:

In which account(s) have you qualified an opportunity?
Is there a name for the opportunity (i.e., code name, project name or program umbrella)?
Given what you know, how large do you estimate the opportunity to be (S, M, L or $)?
What is/are the CBIs that we are addressing?
What product(s)/solution best address the CBI?
How many people are impacted by the CBI? (Demand Organization Charts here …)
Who are the highest ranking executive impacted by the CBI? What is the chain of command?
Who holds the Power to say 'yes'? Who holds the Power to say 'no'?
What is the status of our relationships with those mentioned above?
What is the compelling event that is driving this decision (what makes it imminent)?
What is our unique value? What are our weaknesses? (Solution Fit and Business Value)
Who are the Competitors? (If non-traditional, are we justified in pursuing this?)
What is the Competitor's Strategy? How, and with whom, are they positioned?
Where are our obstacles to making progress in this opportunity (internal and external)?
Who is on our Selling Team, and how do we plan to communicate and stay in synch?
What is our tactical Activity Plan to execute on, and fill-in missing, information?

This last question when building the Opportunity Strategy ("*What is our tactical Activity Plan to execute on, and fill-in missing, information*") is a separate area of focus when conducting a Sales Audit: does the sales manager have a process for developing and assigning specific action items to move the deal to closure? It is execution and feedback on these action items that will result in a win or a loss of the sale.

Chapter 10

Action Planning

Audit Point: Opportunities must be tracked through the Sales Process in order to provide visibility into the actions being taken to keep the opportunities moving towards closure.

Control Document: Call Sheet, 5P Sheet, Opportunity Strategy, Pipeline Management Document, and Action Plan

Prospecting to identify many concurrent opportunities is the name of the selling game, and sales managers must have a simple way to examine the opportunities and progress being made by salespeople. Performing a Sales Audit ensures that processes are in place to qualify multiple opportunities (using Call Sheets and/or the 5P Sheet) to identify what is *known and unknown* about those opportunities and build appropriate execution strategies using the Opportunity Strategy Templates. *Now the Sales Audit examines how to use a Pipeline Management Document to formulate Action Plans for documenting each execution step.*

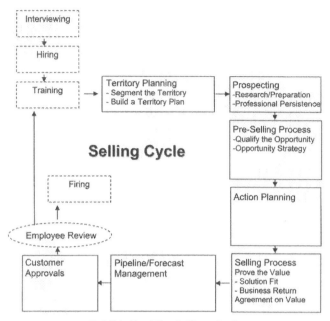

Exhibit E—The Selling Cycle

The Action Plan has five extremely important purposes in managing multiple sales opportunities:

1) To keep each opportunity moving through the Sales Process
2) To document progress and allow for mid-course corrections
3) To give management visibility into the progress of the opportunities and simplify management reviews of the salesperson's performance
4) To keep the selling team (product development, customer support, etc.) in sync with the progress of the opportunities
5) As a 'status document' for keeping the Customer in sync with the progress of the plan (it will make asking for the contract more natural as the salesperson approaches the closing stage in the sales process).

Action Plans put owners and timeframes to the tasks of gathering the information required to complete each stage of the sales process as defined in the Pipeline Management Document. The Pipeline Management Document (**Exhibit S**) details each stage in the sales cycle through which an opportunity must pass (including qualification and legitimization) and the criteria that must be met in each stage before moving on:

Pre-Selling Process (0 - 10%)

Qualifying the Opportunity (0%)
- Pain Identified and Quantified
- Power Identified
- Process for Addressing the Pain Identified
- Preference for a Solution Uncovered
- Plan for Next Steps Agreed Upon

Building the Strategy (10%)
- Strategy Template Complete
- Action Plan Complete

Selling Process (25 - 50%)

Prove the Value - Solution Fit (25%)
- Requirements for Solution Defined
- Prioritize Solution Requirements
- Demonstrate Solution Meets Requirements
- Validates Solution Meets Requirements
- Document Points-of-Differentiation (Solution)

Prove the Value - Business Return (50%)
- Executive Confirms Business Value
- Ballpark Pricing and Budget
- Quantify Business Value (ROI)
- Document Points-of-Differentiation (Business)
- References Checked
- Executive/Corporate Visit

Customer Approvals (75% - 99%)

Vendor Selection (75%)
- Formal Proposal
- Confirm Vendor Selection
- Business and Legal Contract Review
- Define Contract Signature Process

Contract Completion (99%)
- Final Contract Negotiations
- Contract Signature
- Solution Pre-Planning Meeting

Exhibit S—Pipeline Management Document

In order for an opportunity to progress through the sales process as defined in the Pipeline Management Document, each of the 'checkboxes' in each stage must be completed (or, if skipped, logically explained). *Finding the information to complete any unknown 'checkbox' on the Pipeline Management Document will become the tasks (one for each unknown element) on an Action Plan.*

Let's take a look at each stage of the Pipeline Management Document and how the sales manager can help a salesperson use the document to build the Action Plan for an opportunity:

Pre-Selling Process			
Qualifying the Opportunity		Opportunity Strategy	
Pain		Strategy Template	
Power		Action Plan	
Process			
Preference			
Plan			

Pipeline Management Document/Pre-Selling Process Stage

When an opportunity is in the Pre-Selling Process stage, it is being qualified using the Call Sheet and/or 5P Sheet, each aimed at making sure that the opportunity is linked to significant pain, and that someone in a position of power needs urgently to eradicate it. Once qualified, a Strategy Template is built to further legitimize the opportunity by identifying known/unknown aspects of the opportunity. *Until an opportunity is qualified and legitimized, it would be pointless to build an Action Plan for moving it through the selling process.*

Once an opportunity is qualified and legitimized, the salesperson must build an Action Plan by *looking forward* in the Pipeline Management Document to the Selling Process stage, and anticipating the tasks necessary to complete in order to keep the opportunity moving:

Selling Process			
Prove the Value - Solution Fit		Prove the Value - Business Return	
Requirements for Solution Defined		Executive Confirms Business Value	
Prioritize Solution Requirements		Ballpark Pricing and Budget	
Demonstrate Solution Meets Requirements		Quantify Business Value (ROI)	
Validates Solution Meets Requirements		Document Points-of-Differentiation (Business)	
Document Points-of-Differentiation (Solution)		References Checked	
		Executive/Corporate Visit	

Pipeline Management Document/Selling Process Stage

For each 'checkbox' criteria for the 'Prove the Value—Solution Fit' stage that is unknown …

- Requirements for Solution Defined
- Prioritize Solution Requirements
- Validate Solution Meets Requirements
- Document Points-of-Differentiation (Solution)

A task is entered in the Action Plan:

Task	Date	Continue*	Responsibility	Complete
Meeting with Highest Ranking Officer to Validate Value Propositions, Ballpark Pricing, and Budget. Extend Invitation to a Corporate Visit.	10-Oct	*	Us/Dynaco	X
Meeting with Sponsor to Review and Prioritize Technical Requirements. Share Ballpark Pricing.	12-Oct	*	Us/Dynaco	X
Customized Product Demonstration to Decision Committee around Technical Requirements; Submit Customer Reference Examples and discuss any Additional Proof Requirements.	19-Oct	*	Us/Dynaco	X
Post-Demonstration Review with Sponsor to Validate Product meets Minimum Technical Requirements, and to Identify Unique Technical and Business Value. Confirm no additional Proof Points	21-Oct	*	Us/Dynaco	X
Confirm Decision Committee has contacted References. Confirm Technical Win.	25-Oct	*	Us/Dynaco	
Meet with Sponsor to Quantify Business Value and begin Building ROI. Extend Offer for Visit by our Executive or Visit to Corporate.	27-Oct		Us/Dynaco	
Prepare Initial Proposal, including Unique Technical Value, Business Value and Pricing.	27-Oct		Us	

Initial Tasks of an Action Plan

The tasks above are not taken verbatim from the Pipeline Management Document. Grouping (for example, accomplishing multiple tasks within the same meeting with a single contact), sequence, date of completion, and detail behind these tasks will be entirely based on the selling situation. The salesperson should use the Pipeline Management Document as a guide for making certain that the 'check box' criteria for moving an opportunity through the selling process are being 'checked off'. The actual tasks and resulting Action Plan will need to be 'personalized' by the salesperson based on what they know of the company, personalities, timeframes and other 'environmental' aspects of the situation.

Some examples of how the situation can alter the specific task to be added to the Action Plan:

Example 1:

Criteria from the Pipeline Management Document, 'Selling Process/Prove the Value—Business Return' stage (shown above):

Executive Confirms Business Value
Ballpark Pricing and Budget
Executive/Corporate Visit

Actual task from the Action Plan (**first task** in the Action Plan above):

Meeting with Highest Ranking Officer to Validate Value Propositions, Ballpark Pricing and Budget. Extend Invitation to a Corporate Visit.

Three separate criteria in the 'Prove the Value—Business Return' stage have been combined into a single Action Plan task. This is based on having an executive meeting already scheduled, and having knowledge that access to the executive is limited enough that all three need to be accomplished in a single meeting (if possible).

Usually ballpark pricing should be postponed until the salesperson has 'Quantified Business Value (ROI)' (a criteria in the next selling stage: 'Prove the Value—Business Return'). This allows sales management and salespeople the opportunity to base pricing on a fair-value-exchange. However, our knowledge of the customer's unwillingness to proceed with evaluating our solution without some idea of cost forces us to discuss ballpark pricing with the executive earlier than is typical.

Example 2:

Criteria from the Pipeline Management Document, 'Selling Process/Prove the Value—Business Return' stage (shown above):

Quantify Business Value (ROI)

Actual task from the Action Plan (**sixth task** in the Action Plan above):

Meet with Sponsor to Quantify Business Value and begin Building ROI. Extend offer for Visit by our Executive Sponsor or Visit to Corporate.

Although the criteria to 'Quantify Business Value (ROI)' falls just below 'Ballpark Pricing and Budget' on the Pipeline Management Document, actually completing the 'checkbox' falls a full <u>five steps later</u> in the Action Plan. The salesperson needs to have the customer put specific metrics to the business value expected from the solution or, at a minimum, gain customer agreement that the demonstration (in the 'Prove the Value— Solution Fit' stage) actually showed the potential for significant business return.

Example 3:

Criteria from the Pipeline Management Document, Selling Process/'Prove the Value—Business Return' stage (shown above):

References Checked

Actual task from the Action Plan (**fifth task** in the Action Plan above):

Confirm Decision Committee has contacted References. Confirm Solution Fit.

This customer has the requirement to speak with a customer prior to making a decision. Not all customers will require such a task. When performing a 'Reference Check', the salesperson may also need to add a task that includes pre-screening any potential references for 'appropriateness' (company size, vertical market, solution use case, what they'll actually say, etc.).

When each task is complete, an 'X' is logged in the box to the right of the task on the Action Plan. When each task is complete (or the salesperson has convinced management that the criteria is not applicable to this opportunity based on the selling situation), then the salesperson can look ahead to the next stage of the sales process and build the next set of tasks into the Action Plan. [Note: It is the sales manager's choice to have the salesperson cease building out the Action Plan any further until the initial tasks are complete. It will be dependent on the complexity of the opportunity and the capabilities of the salesperson to actually execute a number of complex tasks]

Continuing to look forward in the Pipeline Management Document to the Customer Approvals stage:

Customer Approvals		
Formal Proposal	Final Contract Negotiations	
Confirm Vendor Selection	Contract Signature	
Business and Legal Contract Review	Solution Pre-Planning Meeting	
Define Contract Signature Process		

Pipeline Management Document/Customer Approval Stage

The 'checkbox' criteria for the 'Customer Approvals' stage:

- Formal Proposal

- Confirm Vendor Selection
- Business and Legal Contract Review
- Define Contract Signature Process

For each criteria that is determined to be 'unknown', a task is added to the previous tasks in the Action Plan:

Task	Date	Continue*	Responsibility	Complete
Meeting with Highest Ranking Officer to Validate Value Propositions, Ballpark Pricing, and Budget. Extend Invitation to a Corporate Visit.	10-Oct	*	Us/Dynaco	X
Meeting with Sponsor to Review and Prioritize Technical Requirements. Share Ballpark Pricing.	12-Oct	*	Us/Dynaco	X
Customized Product Demonstration to Decision Committee around Technical Requirements; Submit Customer Reference Examples and discuss any Additional Proof Requirements.	19-Oct	*	Us/Dynaco	X
Post-Demonstration Review with Sponsor to Validate Product meets Minimum Technical Requirements, and to Identify Unique Technical and Business Value. Confirm no additional Proof Points	21-Oct	*	Us/Dynaco	X
Confirm Decision Committee has contacted References. Confirm Technical Win.	25-Oct	*	Us/Dynaco	
Meet with Sponsor to Quantify Business Value and begin Building ROI. Extend Offer for Visit by our Executive or Visit to Corporate.	27-Oct		Us/Dynaco	
Prepare Initial Proposal, Including Unique Technical Value, Business Value and Pricing.	27-Oct		Us	
Engage Customer's Legal Team to Begin Initial Contract and Pricing Review; Exchange subsequent Drafts via e-mail. Define Process for Signature and P.O. Generation	1-Nov		Us/Dynaco	
Review Initial Proposal with Sponsor; Exchange subsequent Drafts via e-mail until Final Draft is acceptable.	1-Nov		Us/Dynaco	
Executive Visit w/Customer Highest Ranking Officer	11-Nov	*	Us/Dynaco	
Review Final Proposal with Sponsor and Highest Ranking Officer	18-Nov	*	Us/Dynaco	
Customer Confirms Final Vendor Selection	20-Nov	*	Dynaco	
Final Contracts in Signature Process; P.O. entered into System	22-Nov		Dynaco	
Signed Contracts and P.O. Received	30-Nov		Dynaco	
Tentative Kickoff and Installation Session Date	1-Dec		Us	

Final Action Plan

Again, the tasks above are not taken verbatim from the Pipeline Management Document. The actual tasks and resulting Action Plan will need to be 'personalized' by salesperson with some help from sales management based on what they know of the company, personalities, timeframes and other 'environmental' aspects of the situation. Continuing the example of how the situation can alter the specific tasks added to the Action Plan:

Example 4:

Criteria from the Pipeline Management Document, 'Customer Approvals' stage (shown above):

Formal Proposal

Actual task(s) from the Action Plan (**ninth and eleventh task(s) in Exhibit S** above):

Review Initial Proposal with Sponsor; Exchange subsequent Drafts via e-mail until Final Draft is acceptable … and …

Review Final Proposal with Sponsor and Highest Ranking Officer

This customer situation demands several drafts of the proposal and reviewing each with the customer prior to presenting a final version. Initial versions of the proposal will explain the value of the solution (business value and financial return), but may still include only ballpark pricing that was shared with the customer earlier (based on customer need to know cost prior to continuing their evaluation of the solution). After review of initial versions with customer sponsors, the final version of the proposal will likely include important changes (for example, fair-value-exchange pricing that will be different from ballpark pricing). This final version is then presented to the highest ranking officer as the final step prior to receiving approval.

Example 5:

Criteria from the Pipeline Management Document, 'Customer Approvals' stage (shown above):

Confirm Vendor Selection

Actual task(s) from the Action Plan (**twelfth task in Exhibit S** above):

Customer Confirms Final Vendor Selection

This is a good example of one criterion from the Pipeline Management Document that won't vary much because it is so critical. The customer should document that the solution is the best overall fit and why. Without it, the customer will have a difficult time selecting a solution objectively, and justifying their selection to executive management.

The salesperson and sales management have leveraged their sales process, as defined in the Pipeline Management Document, to build a complete Action Plan for an opportunity. A similar Action Plan must be built for *every concurrent opportunity that is qualified and legitimate.*

[Note: In Chapter 12 we will discuss how the Pipeline Management Document, used as a guideline for building Action Plans, will also be used to forecast the closure of multiple, concurrent opportunities.]

Chapter 11

The Selling Process: Prove the Value

Audit Point: The company must have a sales process that is documented (Exhibit R—Pipeline Management Document in Chapter 10). The stages for proving solution fit and business return are critical and must be included in the sales process.

Control Document: Pipeline Management Template.

Sales managers know that the sales process truly begins once an opportunity is qualified and legitimate. They also know that once an opportunity is qualified, and an Opportunity Strategy and Action Plan are built, the real work of proving the value of the solution begins.

Exhibit E—The Selling Cycle

The Sales Audit validates that the sales process exists, is documented, and includes very specific tasks for proving the value of the solution within the process. Referring to the sales process documented in the Pipeline Management Document, value is proved in the Selling Process stage:

Selling Process				
Prove the Value - Solution Fit		**Prove the Value - Business Return**		
Requirements for Solution Defined		Executive Confirms Business Value		
Prioritize Solution Requirements		Ballpark Pricing and Budget		
Demonstrate Solution Meets Requirements		Quantify Business Value (ROI)		
Validates Solution Meets Requirements		Document Points-of-Differentiation (Business)		
Document Points-of-Differentiation (Solution)		References Checked		
		Executive/Corporate Visit		

Pipeline Management Document/Selling Process Stage

The Selling Process stage breaks down into two sub-stages:

1. Prove the Value—<u>Solution Fit</u>: the activity required to define the customer's requirements for a solution, document and prioritize them, and show that the solution addresses them.

2. Prove the Value—<u>Business Return</u>: show that the solution's ability to address the requirements outweighs the cost of buying and implementing the solution.

Prove the Value—Solution Fit

A Critical Business Issue (CBI) is a business (or perhaps personal) pain solved through acquiring a product or service. In order to translate how the product or service removes the pain, the pain needs to be broken into "symptoms" that identify the "root cause" of the pain.

I was one of the quickest middle-linebackers on my sophomore high school football team. One week, however, I just wasn't as agile and couldn't practice at full speed. My coach noticed, and asked why I was favoring my legs. I told him my shins had been hurting and he told me to go half-speed. I came home each day after practice with increasingly bad pains in my shins. Inquisitive salesperson that my mother was, she asked me a series of questions that would help her understand the "root cause" of my pain:

"Did you get kicked in the shin?" she asked. "No" I said. "Did the pain just start today?" she inquired. "No, about three practices ago" I said. "Did you do anything different three practices ago that you haven't done before? New drills, exercises, stretching?" she asked. "I got new shoes about a week ago" I said. She asked me about the shoes. "What kind of shoes did you get?" she inquired. "They had a pair on sale. They were a little roomy when I tried them on, but I figured that they'd just be that much more comfortable on the field" I replied. My mother then reminded me that I have flat feet, and that shoes that are too wide allow my feet to "flatten out", forcing all of my weight down on the heel bone. That constant pressure on the heel causes shin splints, hence the pain in my shins. I bought new, regular-width shoes, took it easy for a couple of practices, and in a week the pain was gone.

Let's review how my mother, the salesperson, diagnosed the problem:

The pain: shin pain.
The symptoms: inability to practice at full speed.
The root cause: flat feet in wide shoes.
The solution addressing the root cause: regular-width shoes.

This process of breaking a pain into symptoms, and tracing symptoms back to a root-cause is the same in business as it was in the football example:

A sales manager's experiences falling revenues. When pulling the team and their reports together, revenues were growing until a spike occurred six months ago. Since that spike, sales have consistently declined each month. Taking a look at the growth months, it was apparent that a new model of the product was introduced just prior to the growth. Over the months since the spike, the number of units of the new model sold has been falling off compared to sales of the previous model. Customers who purchased the new model in prior months were not coming back. The sales executive pulled the customer service group together and found an increase in customer complaints and returns. The sales executive then pulled the product manager and marketing manager together to explore the idea of having top customers share their experiences with the new model and use the feedback to both fix the problems and build a customer loyalty program to bring upset customers back.

The pain: falling revenues
The symptoms: new product sales declines, increased product returns
The root cause: new product quality
The solution addressing the root cause: fix the quality; add a loyalty program.

These are straight-forward examples with one or two symptoms. When a customer goes looking to remove a pain, they will build a complete list of symptoms (both known and anticipated) in hopes of eradicating the pain and any potential for it to return. These symptoms become the requirements which must be met by any solution purchased to remove the pain. *If the customer refuses or neglects to document the list of symptoms/requirements, it is suspect whether the pain they are feeling is acute enough to spend effort investigating potential solutions.* If the customer insists on providing only verbal requirements, it suggest they may simply feel a tinge of pain (not enough pain to put the effort into developing a complete list of symptoms/requirements), and might be trying to find a quick, low-cost, low-impact solution.

If the customer is serious about the effort to evaluate solutions to eradicate the pain, the prospect will expend great energy to document all symptoms in their description of the pain. The customer will leverage experience of others who have had this pain. They will aggregate information from vendors who offer solutions to the pain and know the symptoms well. So in building a requirements list for evaluating a solution to eradicate their pain, the customer will include their list of symptoms, explore symptoms from other customers with similar pain, and even aggregate vendor information to make certain their list of symptoms to be addressed by the solution is complete.

As a sales manager, it is imperative that you help the salesperson build and prioritize the list of their symptoms/requirements with their customers. Make certain that what the salesperson ends up with is not just an all-inclusive list of customer symptoms, but a list of symptoms that puts their **most intense and immediate symptoms first**. Why? Without documented and prioritized requirements, the salesperson is guessing at the value of the solution to the customer. The salesperson ends up showing that the solution can do *more* than a competitor's solution, rather than demonstrating that the solution can do *exactly* what the customer requires to eradicate the pain. This is akin to a game of 'pin the tail on the donkey'. The target with the customer's requirements is taped on the wall. The salesperson is blindfolded and spun around three times before walking to the wall. Dizzy, but with solution in hand, the salesperson stumbles toward the wall determined to pin the solution as close as possible to the customer's target.

I once had a member of my sales team who was contacted by a prospective client in the entertainment industry. The customer shared their symptoms and interest in the salesperson's solution. Mid-way through the conversation, the customer shared that they already *owned* a competitor's product, but insisted that the competitor couldn't provide the functionality they desperately needed. This was enough to convince the salesperson that providing a series of demonstrations would result in the customer replacing the competitor's product. In doing so, the salesperson learned a great deal:

First, the customer was using the competitor's product in a limited way, and had no idea that if they just opened up another module they owned, they could get the job done. They were uninformed about the technology they already owned.

Second, they had evaluated the salesperson's solution on paper, and had come to the incorrect conclusion that it had unique capabilities beyond those of the competitor. The customer had misinterpreted marketing collateral and had gone so far as to propagate their misinterpretations internally.

The customer asked the salesperson to offer a short-term pilot of his solution to finish their evaluation of 'solution fit'. After the salesperson and I had a discussion, we declined. We did not want to go through the work of "duking it out" on technical functionality, only to spend a bunch of money trying to get the product to do something it wasn't meant to do.

Sales Managers must help salespeople understand that approaching a customer with a solution before documenting and prioritizing the customer's list of requirements leaves the door open to 'vendor confusion'. In lieu of the customer having their own defined, prioritized requirements, the customer is prone to being led by the vendor that offers solutions to the problem. Vendor #1 defines the problem and demonstrates their solution for the customer. Vendor #2 defines the problem and demonstrates their solution slightly differently. Each new vendor offers a new version of what the customer's problem and solution should be, showing compelling new bells-and-whistles with each product demonstration. Because customers have short memories, the last vendor in the door becomes the 'standard' against which each subsequent vendor is evaluated, and the customer falls into 'analysis paralysis', rendering a timely and accurate decision on a solution nearly impossible.

Sales Managers may want to consider a practice we used at one of my previous employers. The sales team developed a library of requirements from the many sales campaigns the team had conducted. The team collected customer's evaluation criteria for each of the products the company sold and aggregated them into a binder that served as a reference when approaching new customers with the same needs. The sales team simply produced the requirements list for the customer in an effort to give them a 'head start' on building their own list. Most of the time, the customer appreciated receiving the requirements list based on the time it saved them. Of course, it gave the sales team providing the requirements a leg up. Simply put, the sales team was able to affect the requirements list and make certain that those unique aspects of our solution became the mandatory and high-priority requirements for the customer, making ours the 'de facto' solution. If a good relationship is in place with the customer, built on trust and credibility, then the customer may choose to "short-circuit" the evaluation process, taking the documented requirements from the sales team's library and making it their own.

More often than not, however, the customer wants to remain unbiased, and is gathering requirements from various parts of the organization in order to appease all potential users. Given this scenario, the customer will also do a significant amount of research to determine the suppliers who are considered leaders in the product space and select multiple vendors to participate in an evaluation. In this case, it is likely that offering a 'library of requirements' to short-circuit the process or speed the evaluation will fall on deaf ears (or at least not become the 'de-facto' standard or 'sole source manifesto'). In this case the best method is to make certain the salesperson dissects and prioritizes the customer's requirements into what can be called their Minimal Technical Requirements (MTRs).

When salespeople help customers distill their symptoms into a list of Minimal Technical Requirements, it levels the playing field between vendors and helps the customer objectively 'ferret-out' the solution that fits best. They help minimize the impact of sexy, 'gee-whiz' bells-and-whistles that may make one solution look better than the next, but have no impact on the customer's real needs. Just remember the last time you went in to buy a mini-van and came out with a two-seater sports car: what you needed and what looked good were divergent, and you ended up buying the wrong 'solution'.

Getting the customer to agree to MTRs, and having the vendors focus their demonstrations on these MTRs, will likely result in all vendors looking about the same when it comes to 'solution fit'. The customer then rightfully cuts those vendors that can't meet the MTR's and considers factors other than solution fit in order to choose the best solution (relationship, price, vendor breadth-of-product, reduced risk of implementation, etc.). This also allows the remaining vendors to best establish a fair-value-exchange for the 'other factors' that differentiate their solutions.

Prove the Value—Business Return

Demonstrating Solution Fit (showing that the product will meet the Minimal Technical Requirements) is dependent on how well you outline the requirements that each of the potential users will have for the solution. Business Return is similar, in as much as you must understand what the company (and not just the decision-maker) is looking for in return on its investment in a solution to remove a specific pain.

As a sales manager conducting sales opportunity reviews, salespeople will often say that the customer "has no formal process for financially justifying the return of the solution they are considering". Salespeople may also say that the customer "doesn't need to financially justify the solution because it is 'already budgeted'". Sales Managers should know that's bunk. The process for justifying expenditures of any kind has been forever changed by a company's need to demonstrate sound financial controls (i.e., Sarbanes-Oxley compliance), and even those procurement folks that have deep tenure with a company are being introduced to new buying and approval processes. The salesperson must consider that regular reviews of budgets are now commonplace. Companies are shifting budget money from less-critical to more-critical projects based on changing business needs. This results in disappearing budgets or more discriminating CFOs saying 'No' to a previously budgeted line-item.

All companies will follow a rigorous process of justifying investments, and the process will differ based on the level of investment required to solve the business pain. Terms like ROI, payback, and IRR are commonplace. Dependent on the kind of business, and the financial pressures that a company is under at any given time, the customer will need to demonstrate some kind of financial return.

Business value is becoming more important than ever, and the salesperson must do their job of determining *how* their customer evaluates expenditures, and *who* is involved in approving it. The CFO typically has models that must be followed (often involving all kinds of information that the buyer must provide, and some information they will require from the vendor), and the financial analysts/procurement managers gather the numbers and enter them into those models to come up with an estimated return that the product will bring to the business. If that return doesn't meet minimum criteria for return (i.e., 6 month payback or IRR of 110%), then it is likely to either be rejected, reworked, or given a back seat to other investments that do. The salesperson must do a better job than the competitor of providing information that feeds the model, or the salesperson's solution (even though it may be a better 'fit') will lose in the long run. Even more importantly, the salesperson should certify there is budget and justification prior to spending time trying to win the battle of Solution Fit.

Generally speaking, your company should be capable of providing ROI information around the investment in a solution. Often this information comes in the form of case studies from clients that are extrapolated, customer models that are generalized for common use, industry analysts who cover the space and have general metrics to consider, or your own hard work to determine those items important to an ROI. This can take the form of cost avoidance, redeployment of personnel (increased productivity), reduced risk, improved market share and other "softer" qualifiable (versus quantifiable) benefits such as improved customer satisfaction or elevated market opinion. What is most important is that the salesperson understands what metrics are important to the client, gears the justification towards those metrics, builds or feeds the customer's model, and then gains agreement that the model is accurate and acceptable. Often customers will discount models or data for models provided by vendors, or they may take the model and just discount the values in it by 50% or more (so be concerned if the salesperson's first blush at business value just barely clears the hurdle of acceptable return).

The key to getting approval for the procurement of the solution is to understand that there are two aspects to demonstrating value to the client: Solution Fit (against their minimal technical requirements) and Business Return (that the investment meets the metrics for return on investment set by the buyer).

The paradox of 'proving value' is that **the most a customer will accomplish in proving value is to show that there is uniformity amongst some of the vendors offering a solution**, (given they choose the right competitors in the space and they do sufficient homework on defining the minimal requirements for solution fit and business return). Once the customer has uniformity amongst a few vendors, the customer will look to price as a tie-breaker (again, given the maturity of the marketplace and comparable competition, there should be little difference here). Last, the customer will look to more esoteric tie-breakers like:

- Relationship (which is the equivalent of saying "I trust you to reduce my risk")
- Demonstrated success in the marketplace (references with similar customers)
- Proven deployment models to reduce cycle time
- Faster time to value and business return

Outside of what the customer considers the "price of entry" (solution fit by meeting MTRs and demonstrated business return through ROI), customers will grasp for any unique value that a vendor can provide. The closer the vendor's relationship is with the customer, the better that vendor will gain the 'trust-factor' and be able to demonstrate those subtleties that make their offer "one of a kind".

So why do vendors fail to prove solution fit and business return? The process focuses solely on solution fit, OR, important people are omitted when defining solution fit and business return requirements.

When the vendor fails to prove value because they are focused solely on solution fit, the result is often a product 'bake-off'. Vendors slug it out in the trenches, feature-to-feature, and ultimately cheapen the value of the solution by showing little difference in 'fit' and making pricing discounts the primary way to show differentiation. It also can result in long, costly proof-processes if the customer happens to be from 'the show-me state of Missouri'. Proofs-of-Concept, Pilots, Trials, Evaluation versions, etc. are difficult to win and often result in no-decision or the conclusion that either product can accomplish the task (only now the cost of sale has gone through the roof).

When the vendor fails to prove value because they omit people from the 'Prove Value' stage, I think an article in the Wall Street Journal showed it best:

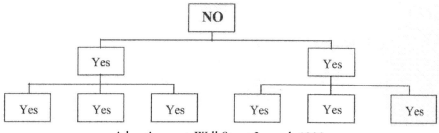

Advertisement, Wall Street Journal, 1992

Everyone in the organization can say yes, but if the highest ranking officer says no, nothing else matters. As the salesperson moves through the strategy and sales processes, sales managers should help the salesperson contemplate the entire organization chart and who is involved (both directly and indirectly) with the issue of solving the pain. The sales manager can be very effective helping the salesperson take time to understand the power structure buried within the organizational chart (who, regardless of title and position, carries weight in the decision process?) and any predispositions people may have that can cause the salesperson to waste time on an opportunity that has already been 'won' by a competitor. Here's an example:

I was working with a salesperson at the highest level within a potential client. She had done a good job of gathering technical requirements, setting the bar for those requirements that became critical to the customer, and understanding the interest, relationships and agenda of multiple players involved in the decision. She orchestrated a flawless demonstration, and the feedback she received was outstanding (even to the point where the customer wanted to hire the person who performed the product demonstration). What we **missed** was that the highest ranking officer had just invested $100M with one of our competitors on an unrelated product, and that he was under mandate by his CFO to justify "*why not*" buy *any* product offered by this competitor instead of sourcing it through someone else. The salesperson's solution fit and business case were turned on their ear, and the value of dealing with a single, incumbent provider (the competitor) far outweighed any solution fit or business value the salesperson had successfully demonstrated. She had failed to identify the *predisposition* of the CFO.

In some cases, salespeople may have identified important people in the process, but have no relationships (i.e., credibility and trust) with them. If there are no relationship at the top of the organization, either the competitor who has them will get the benefit of the doubt when vendor offers start to look the same, or the decision will be left to lower-level staff who will feel the need to break the tie by finding the product bell or whistle that will make the decision easy. A recent example:

A salesperson responded to a 'Request For Information (RFI), only to find days later that he was eliminated from consideration based on his response. He had no relationships anywhere in the organization, and because he was eliminated, his strategy was to go straight to the top to plead his case. He contacted the executive, offering a significant pricing discount on the solution in exchange for an opportunity to speak directly with him about his pain and the solution. To the dismay of the staff (who had eliminated the salesperson's solution after the response to the RFI), the executive granted the meeting. At the meeting, the executive invited that same staff to attend (because he knew nothing of the project, and didn't want to appear uneducated by attending the meeting solo), and the salesperson was ready with his presentation. The presentation focused on the low-risk, no-cost, rapid-time-to-market aspects of the solution (all of which played to the executive's reasons for skepticism towards buying solutions) and consciously minimized the functional specifications of the solution. The executive loved the approach, and after the meeting tasked his staff with implementing the solution and testing it out before they looked at any other vendor's solution. The product implemented just as the salesperson had promised, and the customer bought the product without ever looking at another solution.

This example demonstrates the criticality of having the executive involved in the decision-making, and understanding the requirements of the executive in the role of decision-maker (my disclaimer: the executive should have been involved earlier in the process, and although this example turned into a win, involving an executive after responding to requests from his/her staff is unpredictable and can backfire as often as it works).

The Sales Audit will result in revealing the company's process for helping their customer's prove the value of the solution, both by demonstrating solution fit and business return. Attempting to prove solution fit and business return by performing product demonstrations without pre-defined requirements usually flops. More often than not, it results in spending significant capital (time and money), showing every aspect of the product in hopes of tripping over a feature that strikes a chord with the customer. Such product demonstrations ultimately result in a vendor "beauty pageant": the solution that looks the best on the feature/function catwalk wins. The decision on the winner of a beauty pageant is subjective. The Sales Audit will validate that the company's process is to stick to defined requirements (MTRs) and strong business return justification to even-up the playing field, and then win the opportunity using strong executive relationships and unique 'qualifiable' value (such as risk reduction, references and reduced cycle time).

Agreement on Value

Once the salesperson demonstrates Solution Fit and Business Return, they should gain agreement on the value of the solution and that the value is required immediately. Doing so is essentially just another form of qualification (call it 'triangulation'). The salesperson must get to the highest-ranking executive to validate business pain early in the process, gain agreement that *not* solving the problem will cost the company money, and validate that the company intends to spend money to eradicate the pain (and soon). Through regular sales opportunity reviews, sales managers can build 'triangulation' into virtually every step of the sales process. But certainly it should occur when the salesperson has addressed Solution Fit and Business Return and is looking for the customer to commit to buying. Triangulation should be with the executive who has been engaged throughout the process and has been receiving regular feedback from the salesperson managing the project (if this communication isn't going on regularly it is a bad sign that the problem isn't big enough to concern the executive, which makes the opportunity suspect).

How do you ensure the salesperson gets customer agreement on value? No other way I know of than to hear it directly from the executive, or have our Solution Fit and Business Return cases receive formal sign-off at the executive level. Anything short of that means that the salesperson is taking the word of someone who may not be in the executive 'circle of trust' about the priorities of the business, thus reducing the odds of getting the deal done.

All sales processes should have this triangulation step for agreeing on value. Hopefully, the salesperson has been able to table the issue of price until the agreement on value is reached (since it's this very agreement on value that should drive conversations about price). If the salesperson does an adequate job of proving value and avoiding a formal price proposal, the pricing discussion will be more of a 'fair-value-exchange' conversation rather than a discount-centric hostage situation at the point of closing the sale.

Chapter 12

Pipeline/Forecast Management

Audit Point: Opportunities must be tracked through the Sales Process in order to provide executive visibility into the volume, status and progress of opportunities being managed by each salesperson. Tracking will provide predictability in closure of those opportunities.

Control Document: Pipeline Management Document, Action Plan and Forecast Document

It's time that the Sales Audit turns to pipeline and forecast management:

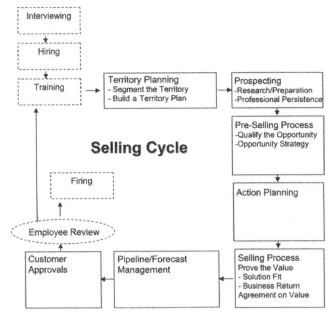

Exhibit E—The Selling Cycle

In Chapter 10, we demonstrated how the Pipeline Management Document (**Exhibit S**) can be used as a guideline for building Action Plans to execute on legitimate opportunities. We also alluded to how it can be used to forecast the closure of multiple legitimate opportunities as they progress through the sales process. *The Sales Audit requires that a process for forecasting multiple opportunities exists, and that the opportunities that are forecasted to close are forecasted based on the stage of the documented sales process they are in at the time of the forecast.* Let's clarify how.

Pre-Selling Process		
Qualifying the Opportunity		**Opportunity Strategy**
Pain		Strategy Template
Power		Action Plan
Process		
Preference		
Plan		

Pipeline Management Document/Pre-Selling Process Stage

When an opportunity is in the Pre-Selling Process stage, it is being qualified using the Call Sheet and/or 5P Sheet, each aimed at making sure that the opportunity is linked to significant pain, and that someone in a position of power is experiencing the pain and needs urgently to eradicate it. Until the opportunity is qualified, it remains in the Pre-Selling Process stage (Qualifying the Opportunity sub-stage) and sales management should have a 0% expectation that the opportunity will close.

Once an opportunity is qualified, an Opportunity Strategy Template is built to identify what is known and unknown about an opportunity and whether that opportunity can be won and closed. If the elements of the Opportunity Strategy Template are satisfactorily asked-and-answered, the qualified opportunity is considered legitimate and the salesperson must build an Action Plan. The Action Plan is assembled by looking forward in the Pipeline Management Document to the Selling Process, and anticipating the tasks to complete and progress the opportunity to closure. The Opportunity Strategy Template indicates the opportunity can reasonably be closed, the Action Plan demonstrates the salesperson's method for progressing the opportunity to closure, and therefore the expectation that the opportunity actually will close is higher than 0%. Given that no actual selling activity has taken place, the sales manager should have an expectation of closure that is ~10%.

When an opportunity hits the Pre-Selling Process stage (Building the Strategy sub-stage), it becomes, for the first time, an opportunity worthy of being 'forecasted to close'. Let's refer back to the Strategy Template built for the Dynaco opportunity as an example:

DynaCo — Data Center Consolidation Project

Deal Size	-	$150,000
Products	-	MXPress
Close Month	-	December

- **Critical BusinessIssue(s), Funding**
  - CIO has committed a FY 7% decrease in hardware capital spending and a 10% decrease in IT expense allocation to CFO
- **Org Charts, Top-Down/Bottom-Up Impact**
  - CIO reports to CFO
  - VP of IT reports to CIO
  - Data Center Manager reports to VP/IT
- **Compelling Event**
  - Budgeting Process completes this quarter
  - 60% of CIO and StaffMBOs rely on results
- **Competition, Predispositions**
  - In-House Consolidation
  - FGH, Incorporated
- **Activity Plan, Decision Criteria**
  - (Attached)

- **Unique Technical Value, Requirements List**
  - Multi-Platform Hardware Consolidation
- **Unique Business Value, ROI**
  - Hardware Re-financing Incentives
- **Issues/Obstacles**
  - Prior Product Challenges
  - Credit Qualification
- **Selling Team Members**
  - Sam Wilson, CFO
  - Regional Solution Partner
  - Professional Services
  - System Engineers
  - Product Management

Exhibit R—Opportunity Strategy Template

The deal size on the Dynaco Strategy Template is $150,000, and the Close Month is estimated as December. Assuming the Dynaco opportunity has moved into the Pre-Selling Process stage (Building the Strategy sub-stage), it would be forecasted as a December opportunity with $150,000 in revenue potential and a 10% probability to close.

Selling Process			
Prove the Value - Solution Fit		Prove the Value - Business Return	
Requirements for Solution Defined		Executive Confirms Business Value	
Prioritize Solution Requirements		Ballpark Pricing and Budget	
Demonstrate Solution Meets Requirements		Quantify Business Value (ROI)	
Validates Solution Meets Requirements		Document Points-of-Differentiation (Business)	
Document Points-of-Differentiation (Solution)		References Checked	
		Executive/Corporate Visit	

Pipeline Management Document/Selling Process Stage

A salesperson with an opportunity in the Selling Process stage has built an Action Plan that includes satisfying the criteria in each of the two sub-stages above. When an opportunity is in the Selling Process stage, the salesperson and customer are in the process of proving whether the solution will fit the customer's requirements and eradicate their pain, and whether eradication of the pain will result in quantifiable business return to the customer. Clearly with every criterion met as solution fit and business return are established, the potential for the opportunity to close increases. The customer continues to demonstrate their commitment to eradicating the pain by spending valuable company resources to investigate the solution, and the salesperson continues to demonstrate how the solution efficiently eradicates the pain and delivers quantifiable value.

When an opportunity is in the Selling Process stage (Prove the Value—Solution Fit sub-stage), the potential for closure increases to ~ 25%. Once the solution is deemed a fit, and the customer is made aware of the cost/benefit analysis and ROI in the Prove the Value—Business Return sub-stage, the potential for closure increases dramatically to ~50%.

Let's again use the Dynaco opportunity and Strategy Template as an example. The opportunity is $150,000, and the Close Month is estimated as December. Assuming the Dynaco opportunity has moved into the Selling Process stage (Prove the Value—Solution Fit sub-stage), it would be forecasted as a December opportunity with $150,000 in revenue potential and a 25% probability to close. If the opportunity moved into the Selling Process stage (Prove the Value—Business Return sub-stage), it would be forecasted as a December opportunity with $150,000 in revenue potential and a 50% probability to close.

Customer Approvals		
Formal Proposal	☐	Final Contract Negotiations
Confirm Vendor Selection	☐	Contract Signature
Business and Legal Contract Review	☐	Solution Pre-Planning Meeting
Define Contract Signature Process	☐	

Pipeline Management Document/Customer Approval Stage

A salesperson with an opportunity in the Customer Approvals stage has built an Action Plan that includes satisfying the criteria in each of the two sub-stages above. When an opportunity is in the Customer Approvals stage, the salesperson and customer are in the process of finalizing a proposal and decision on the solution and vendor, and ultimately moving through the contracts process to closure. Clearly these are critical and definitive steps, and having made it through to these sub-stages the opportunity is not only forecasted, but executive management's expectations are high that this opportunity will close.

When an opportunity is in the Customer Approvals stage (Vendor Selection sub-stage) the potential for closure increases to ~ 75%. Once the customer accepts the proposal, confirms their selection of a vendor, and moves into contract negotiations in the Customer Approvals stage (Contract Completion sub-stage), the potential for closure increases dramatically to ~99%. Very little can de-rail this opportunity, and hence the near perfect percentage for potential closure. The potential for closure of an opportunity reaches 100% only after the salesperson delivers the signed paperwork and the company books the business for revenue recognition. Any time prior always has a 1% potential for a cataclysmic event that can take the chances of closing an opportunity from 100% to 0%. Events such as 9/11, Hurricane Katrina, and Merger/Acquisition activities are all real-life deal-breakers.

Let's again use the Dynaco opportunity and Strategy Template as an example. The opportunity is $150,000, and the Close Month is estimated as December. Assuming the Dynaco opportunity has moved into the Customer Approvals stage (Vendor Selection sub-stage), it would be forecasted as a December opportunity with $150,000 in revenue potential and a 75% probability to close. If the opportunity moved into the Customer Approvals stage (Contract Completion sub-stage), it would be forecasted as a December opportunity with $150,000 in revenue potential and a 99% probability to close.

The success of a salesperson is typically measured by the salesperson's ability to close opportunities as compared to the expectation of executive management. Another measurement of a salesperson's success is the depth of pipeline; the salesperson's 'book of business' (the number of qualified opportunities, where these opportunities fall in the stages of the sales process, and the total potential revenue expected when the opportunities close).

By using the process above, the salesperson and sales management can track progress and performance:

- How many opportunities are in the pipeline?
- How many opportunities are in early stages vs. late stages?
- How much revenue is in the pipeline?
- How much revenue is in early stages vs. late stages?
- Are opportunities and revenue in the pipeline growing?
- Are there specific stages where opportunities seem to stall?
- Do opportunities need a modification to the strategy or Action Plan in order to move them forward in, or eliminate them from, the pipeline?

The Pipeline Management Document, used so successfully for anticipating tasks that must become part of the Action Plan for an opportunity, can be used as a Forecasting Document for multiple opportunities being managed by a salesperson. An example can be found below (**Exhibit T**).

Pre-Selling Process (0 - 10%)

Qualifying the Opportunity (0%)

Pain Identified and Quantified
Power Identified
Process for Addressing the Pain Identified
Preference for a Solution Uncovered
Plan for Next Steps Agreed Upon

Adolph Coors ($100,000)

Building the Strategy (10%)

Strategy Template Complete
Action Plan Complete

Level 3 ($250,000)
J.R. Simplot ($200,000)

Selling Process (25 - 50%)

Prove the Value - Solution Fit (25%)

Requirements for Solution Defined
Prioritize Solution Requirements
Demonstrate Solution Meets Requirements
Validates Solution Meets Requirements
Document Points-of-Differentiation (Solution)

Questar ($50,000)
Utah Power & Light ($75,000)

Prove the Value - Business Return (50%)

Executive Confirms Business Value
Ballpark Pricing and Budget
Quantify Business Value (ROI)
Document Points-of-Differentiation (Business)
References Checked
Executive/Corporate Visit

Motorola ($450,000)
Salt River Project ($25,000)

Customer Approvals (75% - 99%)

Vendor Selection (75%)

Formal Proposal
Confirm Vendor Selection
Business and Legal Contract Review
Define Contract Signature Process

U.S. Airways ($150,000)
Corporate Express ($250,000)

Contract Completion (99%)

Final Contract Negotiations
Contract Signature
Solution Pre-Planning Meeting

Boise Cascade ($300,000)

Exhibit T—Forecast Document

The Opportunity Strategy Template, Action Plan, and Pipeline Management Document are the documents that work hand-in-hand to give salespeople and executive management visibility into productivity they can expect from a salesperson, to perform territory review sessions, and to build a forecast.

Regular opportunity reviews are a common practice by sales managers, but are rarely carried out consistently enough to truly do any good. Managers are too strapped and have too many opportunities to remember the strategies and details of each deal. So instead sales managers tend to ask the same questions quickly and repeatedly in weekly one-on-one sessions with each salesperson:

- Are you still forecasting the deal?
- Is the deal still on track?
- What has changed?
- What is the competition doing?
- What is the next step?

Sadly, the time sales managers tend to uncover details around an opportunity is usually during a loss review …

The Sales Audit examines whether opportunity reviews are happening consistently enough, and include reviewing the previously built Opportunity Strategy Templates and Action Plans and the results from executing on each. The results are what dictate moving to the next step. If the results are different than expected, the sales management and salesperson should determine if the next step should go on as planned, change, or be pre-empted with another step (modifying the documents accordingly). By using this process (without introduction of another document or management tool … trust me, I've seen a boatload of these kinds of 'deal interrogation' documents), the salesperson (who owned the original process of building the Opportunity Strategy Template and Action Plan in the first place) can begin to anticipate the questions that will need to be answered during the next opportunity review and prepare ahead of time so the sessions can be more productive.

Some side benefits of consistent opportunity reviews that include reviewing the previously built Opportunity Strategy Templates and Action Plans:

- The entire team involved in the opportunity can leverage the information on the forms to stay in sync on the steps and results of execution
- Get to the bottom of a competitor's strategy. Who are they talking to? Where are they spending time? Who is their biggest supporter/enemy? What are they telling the customer (we need to anticipate it, and teach the

customer about what they can expect to hear, as it raises credibility when the competitor actually does what the customer is told they will do)? By gathering this information, the opportunity is removed from the bloody battle of product feature vs. product feature, and becomes one of salesperson strategy vs. salesperson strategy.

- Beat the strategy, not the product. The goal being that the salesperson is able to convince the customer that the solution is a safer, wiser choice and not just the cheapest, most highly functioning product on the market

Looking at the Forecast Document (**Exhibit T**), sales management will now have visibility into opportunities even though they are typically not involved in the day-to-day activities surrounding the opportunities. Managers can now be more strategic: helping salespeople to move deals along, see trends regarding where their deals typically stall, use the trends to improve their skills, think about new ways to move the opportunity forward (or kill it if the CBI or urgency has changed), and use the documents to communicate and forecast confidently with executive management.

The true end-result of the sales and forecasting process above is to better predict revenue and when it will hit the books. Predictability is what all sales managers strive for, and this system ensures that surprises are minimized, revenue occurs as it was forecasted to management, future revenue is growing and that the sales team is successful in both delivering revenue and growing the business pipeline.

The performance review is where the detail of how well the salesperson runs the process comes out in the wash.

Chapter 13

The Performance Review

Audit Step: The salesperson must receive regular feedback on their performance. The feedback must be objective based on the results they were recruited to achieve and the results actually achieved.

Control Point: The Performance Review Document.

The performance review is the ribbon to wrap all aspects of the Sales Audit into a nice, closed-loop package. *The Sales Audit will validate that a performance review process exists, is conducted regularly, is objective, and judges success of the salesperson based on the skills determined to be critical during the interview process.* Either the salesperson has utilized these skills to achieve success or the salesperson's success is hampered by the lack of improvement in (or presence of) the skills under review. The sales manager should appreciate that the performance review is 'matter of fact'. Like getting the order after a tightly run sales campaign, the results of a performance review are a natural outcropping of the skills and processes utilized in managing a territory. Because the salesperson's expectations were set from the time of the interview and all throughout the strategy and opportunity review processes (they know how to qualify, they know how to build a strategy, they know and communicate using the tasks in the action plan, and they know how to use the sales process to communicate about opportunities and provide a predictable forecast) the salesperson under review will see it as nothing more than a restatement of how well they executed on expectations. Performance Reviews are best done at the very beginning of a new year, with interim reviews at 6 months.

A review consists of tight synchronization between what skills were verified in the candidate in the interview, and how these skills were applied. An Unconscious Competent (UC, see Chapter 9) that achieved top-drawer results, but has no idea why, is still considered a top performer at most companies. Although they have no idea how they landed the business or why it happened when it did, their review is typically short-and-sweet: 'you've done well, now get out there and do it again'. But sadly, the Unconscious Competent is often unable to duplicate results, and in year two the management team is standing around the water cooler telling 'hero-to-goat' stories about last year's sales leader. In contrast, the salesperson that underperformed according to the numbers, but predicted his performance accurately and kept management informed all year long, is often let go. With them goes the training, product knowledge and customer information to succeed in a company where management will take time to understand the factors that are keeping this salesperson from being the sales leader. For this reason, a performance review has to be organized around the following:

1) Quick Review of Result Metrics (Quota, Margin, etc.).

This is simple and self-explanatory. How has the salesperson delivered on the primary metrics you have for salespeople? The salesperson will rarely debate the results against this metric. They'll have *reasons* for their attainment, but they'll rarely debate the results. The reasons lead us to our next point …

2) Deep Review of Process Execution (how they achieved the results above).

The sales manager should keep a binder of the salesperson's Sales Forecast documents month-to-month over the year. The binder will reveal that opportunities appear and disappear, or that certain opportunities linger within certain stages of the sales process. Select certain opportunities and examine the Opportunity Strategy and Action Plan in the performance review. There is much to tell of the employee's performance by the simple way they have executed the process. Process execution is impossible to fudge. Example:

The salesperson is supposed to keep a full pipeline. When feeling the pressure of a stagnant pipeline, a salesperson typically starts 'relaxing' the qualification process in order to add more opportunities to the pipeline. Most sales managers, not deeply-enough rooted in regular and detailed opportunity reviews, won't be wise to how weak the pipeline is as a result of the unqualified opportunities. But, if performance reviews are regular and include a review of process execution, it will become apparent that the salesperson's opportunities are not 'flowing through' to subsequent selling stages—they are vaporizing before they hit the 'prove value' step due to weak qualification. These are false (unqualified) opportunities, and if the salesperson continues to force them through the steps of the sales process, these opportunities won't close. The review will reveal that the salesperson is having opportunities reach later stages in the sales cycle but isn't closing them, indicating that the salesperson is having difficulty getting the customer to commit. This, in turn, indicates that the salesperson is missing value, missing relationships, missing 'something'. Sales management will be able to track it back to a weak CBI.

Reviewing process execution is a flawless method for quickly identifying where the salesperson is struggling and how to help.

3) Pipeline Growth/Accuracy of Forecasting.

This links to process execution. This is a critical component of the review for the sales manager to keep in mind, and when the pipeline isn't growing or deals aren't closing is usually the time a sales manager calls for a Sales Audit to be performed

4) Tools Utilization

The performance review should examine the use of those templates above deemed appropriate by management for tracking and communicating about sales opportunities. Specific Opportunity Strategy Templates and Action Plan documents should be discussed during the performance review in order to shape any plans for improvement.

5) General Skills

The candidate was tested for certain skills during the interview process. These skills were specific, and specific examples of where the skills were/were not applied throughout the year should be noted in the performance review. An improvement plan should be built for those skills identified as 'weak'.

6) Career Advancement Roadmap.

Based on information above, be prepared to discuss the salesperson's personal goals, and, based on performance, design a roadmap to help them get there.

Below is an example of a Performance Review Document (**Exhibit U**) that includes each of the items above:

Candidate: _____

Interviewer: _____
Interview Date: _____

Skill Strength

Strong ← → Weak

Comments:

Performance Skills:

History of Performance Against Quota
Sales Process Execution
Tools Utilization
Pipeline Growth
Accuracy of Forecasting

General Selling Skills:

Accountability
Ability to Convey Value to Customer
Perceptive to Customer Needs
Verbal and Written Communications
Decision Making and Problem Solving
Recognition and Handling of Objections
Juggling Tasks and Managing Chaos

Total Overall Rating:

Recommendation:

Hire _____   Not Hire _____

Reasons for Recommendation:

Exhibit U—Performance Review Document

Note a couple of things: First, the skills under performance review in **Exhibit U** are the **same areas as the skills tested in the interview questions in Exhibit B**. Not only are interview candidates impressed by the company having the necessary skills outlined and tested in the interview, but by following this 'closed loop' process, employees know that the company is serious about them having, being trained in, and tracking the use of the skills they were hired for.

As a sales manager giving the performance review, make absolutely certain you do your homework and have specific examples of the 'strength or weakness' of certain skills. Use Strategy Templates, Action Plans, and Forecast Documents over time to put color to the points. Any good salesperson will recognize when you are giving off-the-cuff comments and broad generalizations, which can put the validity of the entire review process (and result) at risk.

The Performance Review Document audits the results at each step of the selling cycle, and there is an opportunity to improve salesperson skills and performance in the future in areas where there is a 'disconnect' between expectation and performance. Like the Sales Audit itself, the Performance Review is modular, allowing independent evaluation and improvement to be made at each separate stage. The final performance 'grade' is a defendable outcome of "auditing" each salesperson's ability to carry-out pre-defined skills in a pre-set process.

Conclusion

IBM's sales training program taught me the architecture of a solid presentation:

- Tell 'em what you're gonna tell 'em
- Tell 'em
- Tell 'em what you told 'em

Give the Introduction, then the Presentation, and finally the Conclusion that essentially restates the Introduction (in fact, in IBM Sales School, if the last slide in your presentation wasn't exactly the same as your first slide, you failed …). Well in this case, I'll spare you a full reprint of the Introduction. However, I made two points in the introduction that I want to make sure we accomplished in the book:

1) I asked you to categorize this book as a 'system for *interrogating* your sales process, and improving your results, and the *predictability* of your results, by making your process more *repeatable*'.
2) This book was to walk through the process of the Sales Audit: establish company expectations of the sales team and processes and identify gaps; interrogate the steps of the current sales process and build-in repeatability; and ensure that the process is followed and audited by reviewing performance predictability and results of the process

We have clearly interrogated the sales process from the very beginning, and made certain that the skills expected by the executives are used as the basis for interviewing, segmenting territories, building selling strategies, qualifying and tracking opportunities, and measuring salespeople. I've broken down each of the steps so that your company can look selectively at the areas they deem 'broken' without impacting those parts of the process that are working well. As you review each chapter, there are many tools intricately woven together to give companies more visibility and control of their entire end-to-end selling process. Hopefully, a great many leaders-of-sales will now have the single system (and place to refer back) to build a repeatable process that gives predictability to revenue.

As for the Company leadership, the Sales Audit accomplishes for the sales organization what the Sarbanes-Oxley Audit accomplishes for the corporation: it verifies that the sales management and salespeople …

- Have a consistent and repeatable process for every aspect of running the 'business of sales', from hiring sales talent to grading sales performance
- Have documented these processes for reference by existing and future employees
- Have standardized on these processes and associated tools/systems across the entire sales team
- Are using and following the processes consistently
- Produce predictable results when implementing the process consistently
- Can enforce the use of these processes
- Have proven these processes to be repeatable, opportunity after opportunity
- Have proven these processes to be auditable through opportunity reviews and performance reviews
- Are documenting changes and modifications to the processes, implementing change appropriately (upon approval of senior sales management and after training on new aspects of the selling process) in order to improve their processes over time.
- Have processes that are 'closed loop': the skills we test for in interviews with sales talent are the same skills we grade that sales talent on after they've performed as an employee in a territory.

And just as after the completion of a Sarbanes-Oxley audit, I wish you well in continuing to improve the performance of your company, and in gaining control over the predictability of your business.

Credits and Sources

IBM is a registered trademark of International Business Machines

"EDS Cat Herders" and "EDS Airplane" from Duncan's TV Ad Land—TV Ads, Commercials, Adverts, Videos Online found and reviewed by Duncan Macleod. Original Advertisement by Electronic Data Systems, January 2000 http://www.duncans.tv/2005/

Behavior Profile Results from "Specific Personality Factors" by Corporate Psychology Resources/TalentQuest. Adapted and Used with Permission.

Adolph Coors, Level (3), Questar, Motorola, Boise Cascade, Salt River Project, U.S. Airways, Corporate Express, Utah Power and Light, J.R. Simplot are all registered trademarks of their respective companies.

"To Our Stockholders" from the Level (3) Communications, Inc. 2003 Annual Report, pages 1–7.

The 5P's for Running a Sales Call adapted from "Reading Accounts and Deploying Appropriate Resources (R.A.D.A.R.)" Copyright © 1995 by The Complex Sale, Inc. (www.complexsale.com). Used with Permission.

Conscious Competence Learning Model from "Human Performance and Productivity, Vol. 2: Information Processing and Decision Making", W.C. Howell and E.A. Fleishman (eds.), Hillsdale, NJ: Erlbaum; 1982.

"Advertisement" from The Wall Street Journal, 1992

About the Author

Corey Hutchison has held sales and executive sales management roles in fast-growth companies including IBM, Cognos Corporation, Platinum Technology, Mercury Interactive and Computer Associates. He was vice president of sales for Preventsys and Aqueduct, achieving sales and financial goals by securing and managing client partnerships with the Global 2000. He assumed the chief executive position with Aqueduct, and secured investments with top-tier capital investment firms before leading the company to solid financial performance and stability.

Corey is now President of Playbook Training in Southern California, where he lives with his wife and two children. Playbook Training is a company dedicated to education, training and consulting in professional selling, development and improvement of sales processes, and the business and personal effectiveness of executive management.

Corey received his Bachelor's degree from the University Of Notre Dame.

978-0-595-42134-3
0-595-42134-2

Made in the USA
Middletown, DE
24 August 2017